Made | Simple

Slow Cooker Recipes

Material on pages 4, 5, and 6, and recipes on pages 7, 12, 17, 21, 27, 33, 42, 56, 62, 64, 74, 75, 78, 80, 85, 86, 94, 98, 102, 106, 108, 112, 122, 125, 130, 136, 140, 142, 144, 146, 148, 150, 152, 154, and 155 © Sunbeam Products, Inc. doing business as Jarden Consumer Solutions. All rights reserved. All other material and recipes © Publications International, Ltd.

The RIVAL® logo, Rival®, the CROCK-POT® logo, and Crock-Pot® are registered trademarks of Sunbeam Products, Inc. used under license. Distributed by Publications International, Ltd.

Pictured on the front cover: Asian Ginger Beef over Bok Choy (page 78).
Pictured on the back cover: Sausage & Swiss Chard Stuffed Mushrooms (page 18).

Photography on pages 7, 9, 11, 13, 15, 19, 20, 21, 23, 25, 29, 31, 35, 37, 39, 41, 43, 45, 47, 49, 53, 55, 57, 59, 63, 65, 69, 71, 73, 75, 77, 79, 83, 84, 85, 87, 89, 95, 97, 101, 103, 105, 107, 109, 111, 113, 115, 117, 119, 121, 123, 124, 125, 127, 129, 131, 133, 134, 137, 139, 143, 145, 147, 149, 151, 153, 155, and 156 by Stephen Hamilton Photographics, Inc., Chicago.

Photographers: Tate Hunt, Jennifer Marx
Photographers' assistants: Alison Lazard, Chris Gurley
Prop stylist: Tom Hamilton
Food stylists: Kim Hartman, Mary-Helen Steindler
Assistant food stylist: Sheila Grannen
Recipe developers: Bev Bennett, Nancy Hughes, Marina McLeod, Alison Reich

ISBN-13: 978-1-4127-2586-6
ISBN-10: 1-4127-2586-0

Manufactured in China.

8 7 6 5 4 3 2 1

Microwave Cooking: Microwave ovens vary in wattage. Use the cooking times as guidelines and check for doneness before adding more time.

Preparation/Cooking Times: Preparation times are based on the approximate amount of time required to assemble the recipe before cooking, chilling, or serving. These times include preparation steps such as measuring, chopping, and mixing. The fact that some preparation and cooking can be done simultaneously is taken into account. Preparation of optional ingredients and serving suggestions is not included.

contents

18

40

144

slow-cooking hints and tips

HOW TO GET THE BEST RESULTS FROM YOUR **CROCK-POT®** SLOW COOKER

Your **Crock-Pot®** slow cooker can be the best kitchen assistant you've ever had. Your family will enjoy delicious meals, while you save time and effort, thanks to the flavorful cooking process that works while you're away from home.

Your **Crock-Pot®** slow cooker can also help you entertain guests. It makes a great server for hot beverages, appetizers, or dips. Just keep it on the WARM setting to maintain the proper serving temperature.

To get the most from your **Crock-Pot®** slow cooker, keep the following hints and tips in mind.

Stirring

Due to the nature of slow cooking, there's rarely a need to stir the food unless the recipe method says to do so. In fact, taking the lid off to stir food causes your **Crock-Pot®** slow cooker to lose a significant amount of heat, which extends the cooking time required. Therefore, it's best not to remove the lid for stirring.

Adding Ingredients at the End of the Cooking Time

Certain ingredients are best added toward the end of the cooking time. These include:

- Milk, sour cream, and yogurt: Add during the last 15 minutes.
- Seafood and fish: Add during the last 15 to 30 minutes.
- Fresh herbs: Fresh herbs such as basil will darken with long cooking, so if you want

colorful fresh herbs, add those during the last 15 minutes of cooking time or directly to the dish just before serving it.

Pasta and Rice

For slow-cooked rice dishes, converted rice holds up best through longer cooking times. Most recipes suggest adding pasta or rice halfway through the cooking time for the best texture. If the rice doesn't seem completely cooked after the suggested time, add an extra ½ cup to 1 cup of liquid per cup of rice, and extend the cooking time by 30 to 60 minutes.

Cooking Temperatures and Food Safety

Cooking meats in your **Crock-Pot®** slow cooker is perfectly safe. According to the U.S. Department of Agriculture, bacteria in food is killed at a temperature of 165°F. As a result, it's important to follow the recommended cooking times and to keep the cover on your **Crock-Pot®** slow cooker during the cooking process to maintain food-safe temperatures. Slow-cooked meats and poultry are best when simmered gently for the period of time that allows the connective tissues to break down, yielding meat that is fall-off-the-bone tender and juicy.

If your food isn't done after 8 hours when the recipe calls for cooking 8 to 10 hours, this could be due to altitude, extreme humidity, or voltage variations, which are commonplace. Slight fluctuations in power do not have a noticeable effect on most appliances; however, they can slightly alter the cooking times. Always allow your food to continue cooking until it's done.

If you arrive home and find the electrical power service to your home is out, check the **Crock-Pot®** slow cooker immediately. Check the temperature of the contents in the **Crock-Pot®** slow cooker with an instant-read thermometer. If the temperature is above 140°F, you can transfer the contents to a large saucepan or Dutch oven and finish cooking it on a gas range or gas grill. However, if the temperature of the contents is between 40° and 140°F, you should throw the food away.

If the electricity is on when you arrive home, but you can tell by the clocks that your home has been without power, the best thing to do is throw away the food. You'll never know what the temperature of the food was when the power went off or how long it was off; the food may have spent several hours in the danger zone. And, although the food is hot when you get home and looks done, it is better to err on the side of safety and throw it away.

Allow plenty of time for cooking. Remember, it's practically impossible to overcook food in a **Crock-Pot®** slow cooker. You'll learn through experience whether to decrease or increase cooking times for your recipes.

Browning Meat

Meat will not brown as it would if it were cooked in a skillet or oven at a high temperature. It's not necessary to brown meat before slow cooking. However, if you prefer the look and flavor of browned meat, just brown it in a large skillet coated with oil, butter or nonstick cooking spray, then place the browned ingredients into the stoneware and follow the recipe as written.

Herbs and Spices

When cooking with your **Crock-Pot®** slow cooker, use dried and ground herbs and spices, which work well during long cook times. However, the flavor and aroma of crushed or ground herbs may differ depending on their shelf life, and their flavor can lessen during the extended cooking time in the **Crock-Pot®** slow cooker. Be sure to taste the finished dish and add more seasonings if needed. If you prefer colorful fresh herbs, add them during the last 15 minutes of cooking time or to the dish as a garnish. Fresh herbs add both color and flavor to most dishes.

5

Cooking for Larger Quantity Yields

If you want to make a bigger batch in a larger unit, such as a 5-, 6-, or 7-quart **Crock-Pot®** slow cooker, guidelines for doubling or tripling ingredients include:

- When preparing dishes with beef or pork in a larger unit, browning the meat in a skillet before adding it to the **Crock-Pot®** slow cooker yields the best results; the meat will cook more evenly.

- Roasted meats, chicken, and turkey quantities may be doubled or tripled, and seasonings adjusted by half. Caution: Flavorful dried spices such as garlic or chili powder will intensify during long, slow cooking. Add just 25 to 50 percent more spices, as needed, to balance the flavors.

- When preparing a soup or a stew, you may double all ingredients except the liquids, seasonings, and dried herbs. Increase liquid volume by half, or adjust as needed. The **Crock-Pot®** slow cooker lid collects steam, which condenses to keep foods moist and to maintain liquid volume.

- Do not double thickeners, such as cornstarch, at the beginning. You may always add more thickener later if it's necessary.

Cooking With Frozen Foods

You may cook frozen foods in your **Crock-Pot®** slow cooker. For best results, use the following guidelines:

- Add at least 1 cup of warm or hot liquid to the stoneware before placing frozen meat in the **Crock-Pot®** slow cooker.

- Do not preheat the **Crock-Pot®** slow cooker.

- Cook recipes containing frozen meats for an additional 4 to 6 hours on LOW or 2 hours on HIGH.

- Slow-cooking frozen foods requires a longer cook time than fresh foods because it will take longer for the food to come up to safe internal temperatures. Meats also will require additional time to allow them to become tender. If there is any question about

the cooking time, use a thermometer to ensure meats are cooking appropriately.

High-Altitude Adjustments

If you live at an altitude above 3,500 feet, you'll need to make some adjustments when slow cooking. Everything will take longer to cook, so plan for that. Tough meats take longer to become tender at high altitudes—sometimes much longer. Try cooking on the HIGH heat setting instead of LOW. Root vegetables also take longer to cook; for quicker cooking, cut them into smaller pieces than the recipe suggests.

Removable Stoneware

The removable stoneware in your **Crock-Pot®** slow cooker makes cleaning easy. However, the stoneware insert can be damaged by sudden changes in temperature. Here are tips on the use and care of your stoneware:

- Many stoneware cooking inserts are safe for use in a conventional or microwave oven.

- Because all **Crock-Pot®** slow cookers have wrap-around heat, there's no direct heat at the bottom. Always fill the stoneware at least half full to conform to recommended times for best results. Smaller quantities can still be cooked, but cooking times will be affected.

- Don't preheat the **Crock-Pot®** slow cooker. Don't place a cold insert into a preheated base.

- Don't place a hot insert on a cold surface or in the refrigerator; don't fill it with cold water.

- Never place stoneware in the freezer.

- If you place ingredients in the stoneware and refrigerate the stoneware overnight, additional cooking time will be required to cook the food safely and appropriately. If there is any question about the cooking time, use a thermometer to ensure meats have cooked appropriately.

- Don't use the stoneware insert if it's cracked; replace it.

- For further safety tips, please refer to the instruction manual that came with your **Crock-Pot®** slow cooker.

appetizing beginnings

appetizers

warm blue crab bruschetta

4	cups peeled, seeded and diced Roma or plum tomatoes
1	cup diced white onion
2	teaspoons minced garlic
⅓	cup olive oil
2	tablespoons balsamic vinegar
½	teaspoon dried oregano
2	tablespoons sugar
1	pound lump blue crabmeat,* picked over for shells
1½	teaspoons kosher salt
½	teaspoon cracked black pepper
⅓	cup minced fresh basil
2	baguettes, sliced and toasted

Any lump crabmeat may be used for great results.

1. Combine tomatoes, onion, garlic, oil, vinegar, oregano and sugar in **Crock-Pot®** slow cooker. Cover; cook on LOW 2 hours.

2. Add crabmeat, salt and pepper. Stir gently to mix, taking care not to break up crabmeat lumps. Cook on LOW 1 hour.

3. Fold in basil. Serve on toasted baguette slices.

PREP TIME: 10 MINUTES
SERVINGS: 16
LOW: 3 HOURS

■ **Tip:** Add freshness, color and full flavor by adding fresh herbs to foods just before you serve them.

appetizing beginnings

sun-dried tomato appetizer

3 cups chopped onion
3 jars (about 7 ounces each) oil-packed sun-dried tomatoes, drained and finely chopped
3 tablespoons sugar
1 tablespoon minced garlic
 Grated fresh ginger (2-inch piece, peeled)
1 teaspoon herbes de Provence
½ teaspoon salt
½ cup red wine vinegar
1 package (8 ounces) cream cheese
 Fresh basil sprigs, for garnish
 Assorted crackers

1. Place onion, tomatoes, sugar, garlic, ginger, herbes de Provence and salt in 2-quart **Crock-Pot®** slow cooker. Pour in vinegar; stir gently to mix. Cover; cook on LOW 4 to 5 hours or on HIGH 3 hours, stirring occasionally. Let mixture cool before using.

2. To serve, slice cream cheese in half horizontally (use dental floss for clean cut) and separate pieces. Spread ⅓ cup tomato mixture onto 1 cream cheese half. Top with second cream cheese half and spread ⅓ cup tomato mixture on top. Garnish with fresh basil sprigs and serve with crackers. Refrigerate or freeze remaining tomato mixture for future use.

■ **Tip:** Tomato and cream cheese appetizer may be assembled in advance, wrapped and refrigerated until serving time.

steamed pork buns

PREP TIME: 10 MINUTES

SERVINGS: 8

HIGH: 2 HOURS

■ **Tip:** Straight-sided round casserole or soufflé dishes that fit into the **Crock-Pot®** stoneware make excellent baking dishes.

½ container (18 ounces) refrigerated cooked shredded pork in barbecue sauce*

1 tablespoon Asian garlic chili sauce

1 container (16.3 ounces) refrigerated big biscuits (8 biscuits)

Dipping Sauce (recipe follows)

Sliced green onions, for garnish

Look for pork in plain, not smoky, barbecue sauce. Substitute chicken in barbecue sauce, if desired.

1. Combine pork and chili sauce in medium bowl. Split biscuits in half. Roll or stretch each biscuit into 4-inch circle. Spoon 1 tablespoon pork onto center of each biscuit. Gather edges around filling and press to seal.

2. Generously butter 2-quart baking dish that fits inside 5- or 6-quart **Crock-Pot®** slow cooker. Arrange filled biscuits in single layer, overlapping slightly if necessary. Cover dish with buttered foil, butter side down.

3. Place small rack in **Crock-Pot®** slow cooker or prop up baking dish with a few equal-size potatoes. Add 1 inch hot water (water should not come to top of rack). Place baking dish on rack. Cover; cook on HIGH 2 hours.

4. Meanwhile, prepare Dipping Sauce. Garnish pork buns with green onions, if desired. Serve with dipping sauce.

dipping sauce

2 tablespoons rice vinegar

2 tablespoons reduced-sodium soy sauce

4 teaspoons sugar

1 teaspoon toasted sesame oil

1 tablespoon minced green onion, green part only

Combine vinegar, soy sauce, sugar and oil in small bowl. Stir to blend. Sprinkle on green onion just before serving.

creamy seafood dip

PREP TIME: 5 MINUTES

SERVINGS: 6 TO 8

HIGH: 10 TO 15 MINUTES

1 package (8 ounces) pepper-jack cheese, shredded
1 can (6 ounces) lump crab meat, drained
1 pound cooked shrimp, peeled, deveined and chopped
1 cup heavy whipping cream, divided
1 round sourdough bread loaf (about 1 pound)

1. Place cheese in **Crock-Pot®** slow cooker, and turn to HIGH. Add crab, shrimp and ¾ cup cream. Stir well to combine. Cover; cook 10 to 15 minutes or until cheese is melted.

2. Meanwhile, cut off top of bread and hollow out to create bowl. Cut extra bread into large pieces. Place bread bowl on serving plate. Place extra bread around bowl.

3. Check consistency of dip. Stir in up to ¼ cup additional cream, if desired. To serve, pour into bread bowl.

"melt your mouth" hot wings

PREP TIME: 15 MINUTES

SERVINGS: 10 TO 12

LOW: 5 TO 6 HOURS

40 chicken wing drumettes
2 teaspoons creole seasoning
⅛ teaspoon freshly ground black pepper
2 cups hot sauce
4 tablespoons vegetable oil
4 tablespoons vinegar
4 teaspoons honey
4 tablespoons buffalo jalapeño Mexican hot sauce
1 teaspoon crushed red pepper flakes
1 cup blue cheese dressing (optional)

1. Preheat broiler. Coat broiler pan with nonstick spray. Rinse drumettes and pat dry. Sprinkle both sides with creole seasoning and pepper. Broil 6 inches from heat 10 minutes. Turn wings over and broil 10 minutes longer or until chicken is browned and cooked through. Transfer to **Crock-Pot®** slow cooker.

2. Combine remaining ingredients, except dressing, in medium bowl. Pour over chicken. Cover; cook on LOW 5 to 6 hours, stirring every 60 minutes.

3. Serve blue cheese dressing as dipping sauce, if desired.

creamy seafood dip

mini swiss steak sandwiches

PREP TIME: 15 MINUTES

SERVINGS: 16 TO 18

HIGH: 3½ HOURS

■ **Tip:** Browning meat and poultry before cooking them in the **Crock-Pot®** slow cooker isn't necessary but helps to enhance the flavor and appearance of the finished dish.

2   tablespoons all-purpose flour
¼   teaspoon salt
¼   teaspoon black pepper
1¾   pounds boneless beef chuck steak, about 1 inch thick
2   tablespoons vegetable oil
1   medium onion, sliced
1   green bell pepper, cored, seeded and sliced into strips
1   clove garlic, sliced
1   cup stewed tomatoes
¾   cup condensed beef consommé, undiluted
2   teaspoons Worcestershire sauce
1   bay leaf
2   tablespoons cornstarch
2   packages (12 ounces each) sweet Hawaiian-style dinner rolls

1. Coat 5-quart **Crock-Pot®** slow cooker with nonstick cooking spray. Combine flour, salt and pepper in large resealable plastic food storage bag. Add steak and shake well to coat.

2. Heat oil in large skillet over high heat until hot. Add steak and brown well on both sides. Transfer to **Crock-Pot®** slow cooker.

3. Add onion and bell pepper to skillet. Cook and stir over medium-high heat 3 to 4 minutes or until softened but not limp. Add garlic. Cook and stir 30 seconds longer. Pour mixture over steak.

4. Add tomatoes, consommé, Worcestershire sauce and bay leaf. Cover; cook on HIGH 3½ hours or until steak is tender. Transfer steak to cutting board. Remove and discard bay leaf.

5. Blend cornstarch with 2 tablespoons cooking liquid in small bowl until smooth. Stir into cooking liquid in **Crock-Pot®** slow cooker and continue cooking 10 minutes or until thickened.

6. Thinly slice steak against the grain to shred. Return steak to **Crock-Pot®** slow cooker. Add salt and pepper, if desired. Mix well to combine. To serve, split rolls in half and spoon on steak mixture.

raspberry-balsamic glazed meatballs

PREP TIME: 5 MINUTES

SERVINGS: 18 TO 24

HIGH: 2½ HOURS

LOW: 5 HOURS

1 bag (2 pounds 2 ounces) frozen fully cooked meatballs
1 cup raspberry preserves
3 tablespoons sugar
3 tablespoons balsamic vinegar
1½ tablespoons Worcestershire sauce
¼ teaspoon dried red pepper flakes
1 tablespoon grated fresh ginger (optional)

1. Coat 6-quart **Crock-Pot®** slow cooker with nonstick cooking spray. Add frozen meatballs; set aside.

2. Combine preserves, sugar, vinegar, Worcestershire sauce and pepper flakes in small microwavable bowl. Microwave on HIGH (100% power) 45 seconds. Stir; microwave 15 seconds longer or until melted (mixture will be chunky). Reserve ½ cup mixture. Pour remaining mixture over meatballs and toss gently to coat well. Cover; cook on LOW 5 hours or on HIGH 2½ hours.

3. Turn **Crock-Pot®** slow cooker to HIGH. Stir in ginger, if desired, and reserved ½ cup preserve mixture. Cook, uncovered, 15 to 20 minutes longer or until thickened slightly, stirring occasionally.

■ **Serving suggestion:**
To serve as a main dish, toss with chopped green onions and serve over hot rice. Makes 8 main-dish servings.

16

tomato topping for bruschetta

6 medium tomatoes, peeled, cored, seeded and diced
2 celery stalks, trimmed and chopped
2 shallots, chopped
4 pepperoncini peppers, chopped*
2 teaspoons tomato paste
1 teaspoon salt
½ teaspoon black pepper
2 tablespoons olive oil
8 slices country bread or other large round bread
2 cloves garlic

Pepperoncini are pickled peppers sold in jars with brine. They're available in the supermarket condiment aisle.

1. Drain off any tomato juices. Combine tomatoes, celery, shallots, pepperoncini peppers, tomato paste, salt, black pepper and oil in 4-quart **Crock-Pot®** slow cooker. Cover; cook on LOW 45 minutes to 1 hour.

2. Toast bread. Immediately rub with garlic. Spread tomato topping on bread. Serve immediately.

■ **Variation:** To serve as a main dish, omit bread and garlic, and toss tomato topping with cooked penne pasta. You may also spoon the topping over roasted chicken breasts as a flavorful sauce.

PREP TIME: 10 MINUTES

SERVINGS: 8

LOW: 45 MINUTES TO 1 HOUR

best asian-style ribs

2 full racks baby back pork ribs, split into 3 sections each
6 ounces hoisin sauce
2 tablespoons minced fresh ginger
½ cup maraschino cherries
½ cup rice wine vinegar
Water to cover
4 scallions, chopped

Combine ribs, hoisin sauce, ginger, cherries, vinegar and water in **Crock-Pot®** slow cooker. Cover; cook on LOW 6 to 7 hours or on HIGH 3 to 3½ hours, or until pork is tender. Sprinkle with scallions before serving.

PREP TIME: 10 MINUTES

SERVINGS: 6 TO 8

HIGH: 3 TO 3½ HOURS

LOW: 6 TO 7 HOURS

17

sausage & swiss chard stuffed mushrooms

PREP TIME: 20 MINUTES

SERVINGS: 6 TO 8

HIGH: 3 HOURS

■ **Variation:** If desired, place a small square of sliced Swiss cheese on each mushroom and continue cooking 15 minutes longer or until cheese is melted. Proceed as directed.

2 packages (6 ounces each) baby portobello mushrooms *or* large brown stuffing mushrooms*

4 tablespoons extra-virgin olive oil, divided

½ teaspoon salt, divided

½ teaspoon black pepper, divided

½ pound bulk pork sausage

½ onion, finely chopped

2 cups Swiss chard, rinsed and chopped

¼ teaspoon dried thyme

2 tablespoons garlic-and-herb-flavored dried bread crumbs

1½ cups chicken broth, divided

2 tablespoons grated Parmesan cheese

2 tablespoons chopped fresh parsley

*Use "baby bellas" or crimini mushrooms. Do not substitute white button mushrooms.

1. Coat 5- to 6-quart **Crock-Pot®** slow cooker with nonstick cooking spray. Wipe mushrooms clean, remove stems and hollow out mushroom caps. Pour 3 tablespoons oil into small bowl. Brush mushrooms inside and out with oil. Season mushrooms with ¼ teaspoon salt and ¼ teaspoon pepper; set aside.

2. Heat remaining 1 tablespoon oil in medium skillet over medium heat until hot. Add sausage. Cook and stir until browned. Transfer sausage with slotted spoon to medium bowl.

3. Add onion to skillet. Cook and stir, loosening browned bits, about 3 minutes or until onions are translucent. Stir in chard and thyme. Cook until chard is just wilted, about 1 to 2 minutes.

4. Remove skillet from heat. Add sausage, bread crumbs, 1 tablespoon broth, remaining ¼ teaspoon salt and remaining ¼ teaspoon pepper. Mix well to combine. Scoop 1 tablespoon of stuffing into each mushroom cap. Divide remaining stuffing evenly between mushrooms.

5. Pour remaining broth into **Crock-Pot®** slow cooker. Arrange stuffed mushrooms in bottom. Cover; cook on HIGH 3 hours or until mushrooms are tender. To serve, remove mushrooms with slotted spoon; discard cooking liquid. Blend cheese and parsley and sprinkle onto mushrooms.

shrimp fondue

PREP TIME: 15 MINUTES

MAKES: 5 CUPS

LOW: 2 HOURS

1   **pound shrimp, peeled, cleaned and deveined**
½   **cup water**
½   **teaspoon salt, divided**
2   **tablespoons butter**
4   **teaspoons Dijon mustard**
6   **slices thick-sliced white bread, crusts removed***
2   **eggs, beaten**
1   **cup milk**
¼   **teaspoon black pepper**
2   **cups (8 ounces) shredded Gruyère or Swiss cheese**
    Crusty French bread, sliced

*Thick-sliced bread is often sold as "Texas Toast" in supermarket bread aisles.

■ **Tip:** For a party, use a **Crock-Pot®** slow cooker on the low or warm setting to keep hot dips and fondues warm.

1. Coat **Crock-Pot®** slow cooker with nonstick cooking spray. Place shrimp, water and ¼ teaspoon salt in small saucepan. Cover; cook over medium heat about 3 minutes or until shrimp is pink and cooked through. Remove shrimp with slotted spoon, and reserve ½ cup broth.

2. Combine butter and mustard in small bowl. Spread mixture onto bread slices. Cut bread into 1-inch cubes; set aside.

3. Beat eggs, milk, reserved ½ cup broth, remaining ¼ teaspoon salt and pepper in small bowl; set aside.

4. Spread ⅓ of bread cubes in bottom of **Crock-Pot®** slow cooker. Top with ⅓ of shrimp. Sprinkle with ⅓ of cheese. Repeat layering 2 more times. Pour egg mixture over layers. Use rubber spatula to push bread below surface to absorb liquid. Line lid with 2 paper towels. Cover tightly; cook on LOW 2 hours or until mixture is hot, thick and cheesy. Serve with French bread for dipping.

light
meals

orange cranberry-nut bread

2 cups all-purpose flour
1 teaspoon baking powder
½ teaspoon baking soda
¼ teaspoon salt
½ cup chopped pecans
1 cup dried cranberries
2 teaspoons dried orange peel
⅔ cup boiling water
¾ cup sugar
2 tablespoons shortening
1 egg, lightly beaten
1 teaspoon vanilla

1. Coat **Crock-Pot®** slow cooker with nonstick cooking spray. Blend flour, baking powder, baking soda and salt in medium bowl. Mix in pecans; set aside.

2. Combine cranberries and orange peel in separate medium bowl; pour boiling water over fruit mixture and stir. Add sugar, shortening, egg and vanilla; stir just until blended. Add flour mixture; stir just until blended.

3. Pour batter into **Crock-Pot®** slow cooker. Cover; cook on HIGH 1¼ to 1½ hours, or until edges begin to brown and cake tester inserted into center comes out clean. Remove stoneware from **Crock-Pot®** slow cooker. Cool on wire rack about 10 minutes; remove bread from stoneware and cool completely on rack.

PREP TIME: 10 MINUTES

SERVINGS: 8 TO 10

HIGH: 1¼ TO 1½ HOURS

■ **Note:** This recipe works best in a round **Crock-Pot®** slow cooker.

glazed cinnamon coffee cake

PREP TIME: 10 MINUTES

SERVINGS: 6 TO 8

HIGH: 1¾ TO 2 HOURS

■ **Note:** This recipe works best in a round **Crock-Pot®** slow cooker.

streusel

¼ cup biscuit baking mix
¼ cup packed light brown sugar
½ teaspoon ground cinnamon

batter

1½ cups biscuit baking mix
¾ cup granulated sugar
½ cup vanilla or plain yogurt
1 large egg, lightly beaten
1 teaspoon vanilla

glaze

1 to 2 tablespoons milk
1 cup powdered sugar
½ cup sliced almonds (optional)

1. Generously coat 4-quart **Crock-Pot®** slow cooker with butter or cooking spray. Cut parchment paper to fit bottom of stoneware* and press into place. Spray paper lightly with nonstick cooking spray.

2. Prepare streusel: blend ¼ cup baking mix, brown sugar and cinnamon in small bowl; set aside.

3. Prepare batter: Mix 1½ cups baking mix, granulated sugar, yogurt, egg and vanilla in medium bowl until well blended. Spoon ½ of batter into **Crock-Pot®** slow cooker. Sprinkle ½ of streusel over top. Repeat with remaining batter and streusel.

4. Line lid with 2 paper towels. Cover tightly; cook on HIGH 1¾ to 2 hours or until tester inserted in center comes out clean and cake springs back when gently pressed. Allow cake to rest 10 minutes. Invert onto plate and peel off paper. Invert again onto serving plate.

5. Prepare glaze: Whisk milk into powdered sugar 1 tablespoon at a time until desired consistency. Spoon glaze over top of cake. Garnish with sliced almonds, if desired. Cut into wedges. Serve warm or cold.

***To cut parchment paper to fit, trace around the stoneware bottom, then cut the paper slightly smaller to fit. If parchment paper is unavailable, substitute waxed paper.**

ham and cheddar brunch strata

PREP TIME: 10 MINUTES

SERVINGS: 6 TO 8

LOW: 3½ HOURS

■ **Tip:** When preparing ingredients for the **Crock-Pot®** slow cooker, cut into uniform pieces so everything cooks evenly.

8 ounces French bread, torn into small pieces
2 cups shredded sharp Cheddar cheese, divided
1½ cups diced ham
½ cup finely chopped green onions (white and green parts), divided
4 large eggs
1 cup half-and-half *or* whole milk
1 tablespoon Worcestershire sauce
⅛ teaspoon ground red pepper

1. Coat **Crock-Pot®** slow cooker with nonstick cooking spray. Cut parchment paper to fit bottom of stoneware* and press into place. Spray paper lightly with nonstick cooking spray.

2. Layer in following order: bread, 1½ cups cheese, ham and all but 2 tablespoons green onions.

3. Whisk eggs, half-and-half, Worcestershire sauce and red pepper in small bowl. Pour evenly over layered ingredients in **Crock-Pot®** slow cooker. Cover; cook on LOW 3½ hours or until knife inserted into center comes out clean. Turn off heat. Sprinkle evenly with reserved ½ cup cheese and 2 tablespoons green onions. Let stand, covered, 10 minutes or until cheese has melted.

4. To serve, run a knife or rubber spatula around outer edges, lifting bottom slightly. Invert onto plate and peel off paper. Invert again onto serving plate.

*To cut parchment paper to fit, trace around the stoneware bottom, then cut the paper slightly smaller to fit. If parchment paper is unavailable, substitute waxed paper.

24

apple and granola breakfast cobbler

PREP TIME: 5 MINUTES

SERVINGS: 4

HIGH: 2 TO 3 HOURS

LOW: 6 HOURS

4 Granny Smith apples, peeled, cored and sliced
½ cup packed light brown sugar
1 teaspoon ground cinnamon
1 tablespoon lemon juice
2 tablespoons butter, cut into small pieces
2 cups granola cereal, plus additional for garnish
Cream, half-and-half or vanilla yogurt (optional)

1. Place apples in 4-quart **Crock-Pot®** slow cooker. Sprinkle brown sugar, cinnamon and lemon juice over apples. Stir in butter and granola.

2. Cover; cook on LOW 6 hours or on HIGH 2 to 3 hours. Serve hot with additional granola sprinkled on top. Serve with cream, if desired.

savory sausage bread pudding

PREP TIME: 10 MINUTES

SERVINGS: 4 TO 6

LOW: 4 TO 5 HOURS

4 eggs
2 cups milk *or* 1 cup half-and-half and 1 cup milk
¼ teaspoon salt
¼ teaspoon black pepper
¼ teaspoon crushed dried thyme
⅛ teaspoon crushed red pepper flakes
1 package (10 ounces) smoky breakfast sausage links, cut into ½-inch pieces
¾ cup shredded Cheddar cheese
2 cups day-old bread cubes, cut into ½-inch pieces

1. Beat eggs in large bowl. Add milk, salt, pepper, thyme and pepper flakes; stir in well. Stir in sausage, cheese and bread. Press bread into egg mixture. Set aside 10 minutes or until bread has absorbed liquid.

2. Generously butter 2-quart baking dish that fits inside 5- or 6-quart **Crock-Pot®** slow cooker. Pour sausage mixture into baking dish. Cover dish with buttered foil, butter side down.

3. Pour 1 inch hot water into **Crock-Pot®** slow cooker. Add baking dish. Cover; cook on LOW 4 to 5 hours or until tester inserted into center comes out clean.

cheese grits with chiles and bacon

6 strips bacon, divided
1 serrano or jalapeño pepper,* cored, seeded and minced
1 large shallot or small onion, finely chopped
1 cup grits**
4 cups chicken broth
¼ teaspoon black pepper
Salt, to taste
½ cup half-and-half
1 cup shredded Cheddar cheese
2 tablespoons finely chopped green onion, green part only

*Hot peppers can sting and irritate the skin, so wear rubber gloves when handling peppers and do not touch eyes.

**You may use coarse, instant, yellow or stone-ground grits.

1. Fry bacon on both sides in medium skillet until crisp. Remove bacon and drain on paper towels. Cut 2 strips into bite-size pieces. Refrigerate and reserve remaining bacon. Place cut-up bacon in 5-quart **Crock-Pot®** slow cooker.

2. Drain all but 1 tablespoon bacon drippings in skillet. Add pepper and shallot. Cook and stir over medium-high heat 1 minute or until shallot is transparent and lightly browned. Transfer to **Crock-Pot®** slow cooker. Stir in grits, broth, pepper and salt. Cover; cook on LOW 4 hours.

3. Stir in half-and-half and cheese. Sprinkle on green onions. Chop remaining bacon into bite-size pieces and stir into grits or sprinkle on top of each serving. Serve immediately.

PREP TIME: 15 MINUTES

SERVINGS: 4

LOW: 4 HOURS

"wake up to health" cereal

1½ cups steel-cut or old-fashioned oats
3 cups water
2 cups chopped peeled apples
¼ cup sliced almonds
½ teaspoon ground cinnamon

Combine oats, water, apples, almonds and cinnamon in **Crock-Pot®** slow cooker. Cover; cook on LOW 8 hours.

PREP TIME: 10 MINUTES

SERVINGS: 6

LOW: 8 HOURS

oatmeal crème brûlée

PREP TIME: 15 MINUTES

SERVINGS: 4 TO 6

LOW: 3 TO 3½ HOURS

4 cups water
3 cups quick-cooking oatmeal
½ teaspoon salt
6 egg yolks
½ cup granulated sugar
2 cups whipping cream
1 teaspoon vanilla
¼ cup packed light brown sugar
Fresh berries (optional)

■ **Tip:** This rich, sweet dish is delicious for breakfast or lunch, but also can be served as an unusual dessert.

1. Coat **Crock-Pot®** slow cooker with nonstick cooking spray. Cover and set on HIGH to heat. Meanwhile, bring water to a boil. Immediately pour into preheated **Crock-Pot®** slow cooker. Stir in oatmeal and salt. Cover.

2. Combine egg yolks and granulated sugar in small bowl. Mix well; set aside. Heat cream and vanilla in medium saucepan over medium heat until mixture begins to simmer (small bubbles begin to form at edge of pan). *Do not boil.* Remove from heat. Whisk ½ cup hot cream into yolks, stirring rapidly so yolks don't cook.* Whisk warmed egg mixture into cream, stirring rapidly to blend well. Spoon mixture over oatmeal. *Do not stir.*

3. Turn **Crock-Pot®** slow cooker to LOW. Line lid with 2 paper towels. Cover tightly; cook on LOW 3 to 3½ hours or until custard has set.

4. Uncover and sprinkle brown sugar over surface of custard. Line lid with 2 dry paper towels. Cover tightly; continue cooking on LOW 10 to 15 minutes or until brown sugar has melted. Serve with fresh berries, if desired.

Place bowl on damp towel to prevent slipping.

bran muffin bread

PREP TIME: 10 MINUTES

SERVINGS: 12

LOW: 3½ TO 4 HOURS

■ **Tip:** Cooking times are guidelines. **Crock-Pot®** slow cookers, just like ovens, cook differently depending on the recipe size and the individual slow cooker. Always check for doneness before serving.

2 cups all-bran cereal
2 cups whole-wheat flour*
2 teaspoons baking powder
1 teaspoon baking soda
¼ teaspoon ground cinnamon
½ teaspoon salt
1 egg
1½ cups buttermilk
¼ cup molasses
¼ cup (½ stick) unsalted butter, melted
1 cup chopped walnuts
½ cup raisins
Honey butter or cream cheese (optional)

For proper texture of finished bread, spoon flour into measuring cup and level off. Do not dip into bag, pack down flour or tap on counter to level when measuring.

1. Generously butter and flour 8-cup mold that fits into 6-quart **Crock-Pot®** slow cooker; set aside. Combine cereal, flour, baking powder, baking soda, cinnamon and salt in large bowl. Stir to blend well.

2. Beat egg in medium bowl. Add buttermilk, molasses and melted butter. Mix well to blend. Add to flour mixture. Stir only until ingredients are combined. Stir in walnuts and raisins. Spoon batter into prepared mold. Cover with buttered foil, butter side down.

3. Place rack in **Crock-Pot®** slow cooker or prop up mold with a few equal-size potatoes. Pour 1 inch hot water into **Crock-Pot®** slow cooker (water should not come to top of rack). Place mold on rack. Cover; cook on LOW 3½ to 4 hours.

4. To check for doneness, lift foil. Bread should just start to pull away from sides of mold, and toothpick inserted into center of bread should come out clean. If necessary, replace foil and continue cooking 45 minutes longer.

5. Remove mold from **Crock-Pot®** slow cooker. Let stand 10 minutes. Remove foil and run rubber spatula around outer edges, lifting bottom slightly to loosen. Invert bread onto wire rack. Cool until lukewarm. Slice and serve with honey butter, if desired.

wake-up potato and sausage breakfast casserole

1 pound kielbasa or smoked sausage, diced
1 cup chopped onion
1 cup chopped red bell pepper
1 package (20 ounces) refrigerated Southwestern-style hash browns*
10 large eggs
1 cup milk
1 cup shredded Monterey Jack or sharp Cheddar cheese

If unavailable, you may substitute O'Brien potatoes and add ½ teaspoon chili pepper.

1. Coat **Crock-Pot**® slow cooker with nonstick cooking spray. Heat large skillet over medium-high heat until hot. Add sausage and onion. Cook and stir until sausage is browned. Drain and discard excess fat. Stir in bell pepper.

2. Place ⅓ of potatoes in **Crock-Pot**® slow cooker. Top with ½ of sausage mixture. Repeat layers. Spread remaining ⅓ of potatoes evenly on top.

3. Whisk eggs and milk in medium bowl. Pour evenly over potatoes. Cover; cook on LOW 6 to 7 hours.

4. Turn off **Crock-Pot**® slow cooker. Sprinkle on cheese, and let stand 10 minutes or until cheese is melted. To serve, spoon onto plates.

■ **Tip:** For an attractive presentation on a buffet table, display this casserole on a serving plate. To serve this way, omit step 4. Instead, loosen the casserole in the **Crock-Pot**® slow cooker by running a rubber spatula around the outer edges, lifting the bottom slightly. Invert onto a plate. Place a serving plate on top and invert again. Sprinkle with the cheese and let stand until cheese is melted. To serve, cut in wedges.

bacon and cheese brunch potatoes

3 medium russet potatoes (about 2 pounds), peeled and cut into 1-inch dice

1 cup chopped onion

½ teaspoon seasoned salt

4 slices crisply cooked bacon, crumbled

1 cup (4 ounces) shredded sharp Cheddar cheese

1 tablespoon water *or* chicken broth

1. Coat 4-quart **Crock-Pot®** slow cooker with cooking spray. Place half of potatoes in **Crock-Pot®** slow cooker. Sprinkle on ½ of onion and seasoned salt over potatoes; top with ½ of bacon and cheese. Repeat layers, ending with cheese. Sprinkle water over top.

2. Cover; cook on LOW 6 hours or on HIGH 3½ hours, or until potatoes and onion are tender. Stir gently to mix and serve hot.

PREP TIME: 10 MINUTES

SERVINGS: 6

HIGH: 3½ HOURS

LOW: 6 HOURS

hawaiian fruit compote

3 cups coarsely chopped fresh pineapple

3 grapefruits, peeled and sectioned

2 cups chopped fresh peaches

2 to 3 limes, peeled and sectioned

1 mango, peeled and chopped

2 bananas, peeled and sliced

1 tablespoon lemon juice

1 can (21 ounces) cherry pie filling

Slivered almonds (optional)

1. Place all ingredients, except almonds, in **Crock-Pot®** slow cooker and toss lightly. Cover; cook on LOW 4 to 5 hours or on HIGH 2 to 3 hours.

2. Serve with almonds, if desired.

PREP TIME: 15 MINUTES

SERVINGS: 6 TO 8

HIGH: 2 TO 3 HOURS

LOW: 4 TO 5 HOURS

chocolate-stuffed slow cooker french toast

light meals

PREP TIME: 15 MINUTES

SERVINGS: 6

HIGH: 3 HOURS

■ **Tip:** Any oven-safe casserole or baking dish is safe to use in your **Crock-Pot®** slow cooker. Place directly inside the stoneware, and follow the recipe directions.

6 slices (¾ inch thick) day-old challah*
½ cup semisweet chocolate chips, divided
6 eggs
3 cups half-and-half
⅔ cup sugar
1 teaspoon vanilla
¼ teaspoon salt
Powdered sugar or warm maple syrup
Fresh fruit, for garnish

Challah is usually braided. If you use brioche or another rich egg bread, slice bread to fit baking dish.

1. Generously butter 2½-quart baking dish that fits inside 6-quart **Crock-Pot®** slow cooker. Arrange 2 bread slices in bottom of dish. Sprinkle on ¼ cup chocolate chips. Add 2 more bread slices. Sprinkle with remaining ¼ cup chocolate chips. Top with remaining 2 bread slices.

2. Beat eggs in large bowl. Stir in half-and-half, sugar, vanilla and salt. Pour egg mixture over bread layers. Press bread into liquid. Set aside 10 minutes or until bread has absorbed liquid. Cover dish with buttered foil, butter side down.

3. Pour 1 inch hot water into **Crock-Pot®** slow cooker. Add baking dish. Cover; cook on HIGH 3 hours or until toothpick inserted into center comes out clean. Remove dish and let stand 10 minutes to firm up. Serve with powdered sugar. Garnish with fresh fruit, if desired.

apple-cinnamon breakfast risotto

PREP TIME: 10 MINUTES

SERVINGS: 6

HIGH: 1½ TO 2 HOURS

■ **Tip:** Keep the lid on! The **Crock-Pot®** slow cooker can take as long as 30 minutes to regain heat lost when the cover is removed.

4 tablespoons (½ stick) butter
4 medium Granny Smith apples, peeled, cored and diced into ½-inch cubes (about 1½ pounds)
1½ teaspoons ground cinnamon
¼ teaspoon ground allspice
¼ teaspoon salt
1½ cups arborio rice
½ cup packed dark brown sugar
4 cups unfiltered apple juice,* at room temperature
1 teaspoon vanilla
Optional toppings: dried cranberries, sliced almonds, milk

If unfiltered apple juice is unavailable, use any apple juice.

1. Coat **Crock-Pot®** slow cooker with nonstick cooking spray; set aside. Melt butter in large skillet over medium-high heat. Add apples, cinnamon, allspice and salt. Cook and stir 3 to 5 minutes or until apples begin to release juices. Transfer to **Crock-Pot®** slow cooker.

2. Add rice and stir to coat. Sprinkle brown sugar evenly over top. Add apple juice and vanilla. Cover; cook on HIGH 1½ to 2 hours or until all liquid is absorbed. Ladle risotto into bowls and serve hot. Garnish as desired.

french toast bread pudding

PREP TIME: 15 MINUTES

SERVINGS: 6 TO 8

HIGH: 1½ TO 2 HOURS

LOW: 3 TO 4 HOURS

■ **Tip:** Allow breads, cakes and puddings to cool at least 5 minutes before scooping or removing them from the **Crock-Pot®** stoneware.

2	tablespoons packed dark brown sugar
2½	teaspoons ground cinnamon
1	loaf (24 ounces) Texas-toast-style bread*
2	cups whipping cream
2	cups half-and-half
2	teaspoons vanilla
¼	teaspoon salt
4	egg yolks
1¼	cups granulated sugar
¼	teaspoon ground nutmeg
	Maple syrup
	Whipped cream (optional)

If unavailable, cut day-old 24-ounce loaf of white sandwich bread into 1-inch-thick slices.

1. Coat 3½-quart oval **Crock-Pot®** slow cooker with nonstick cooking spray. Combine brown sugar and cinnamon in small bowl. Reserve 1 tablespoon; set aside.

2. Cut bread slices in half diagonally. Using heels on bottom, if desired, arrange bread slices in single layer in bottom of **Crock-Pot®** slow cooker, keeping as flat as possible. Evenly sprinkle on rounded tablespoon of cinnamon mixture. Repeat layering with remaining bread and cinnamon mixture, keeping layers as flat as possible. Tuck bread into vertical spaces, if necessary.

3. Cook and stir cream, half-and-half, vanilla and salt in large saucepan over medium heat, allowing mixture to come to a boil. Reduce heat to low.

4. Meanwhile, whisk egg yolks and granulated sugar in medium bowl. Continue to whisk quickly while adding ¼ cup of hot cream mixture.** Add warmed egg mixture to saucepan and increase heat to medium-high. Cook and stir about 5 minutes or until mixture thickens slightly. *Do not boil.*

5. Remove from heat and stir in nutmeg. Pour mixture over bread and press bread down lightly. Sprinkle reserved cinnamon mixture on top. Cover; cook on LOW 3 to 4 hours or on HIGH 1½ to 2 hours, or until tester inserted into center comes out clean.

6. Turn off **Crock-Pot®** slow cooker and uncover. Let pudding rest 10 minutes before spooning into bowls. Serve with maple syrup and whipped cream, if desired.

***Place bowl on damp towel to prevent slipping.**

thai steak salad

PREP TIME: 15 MINUTES

SERVINGS: 4 TO 6

HIGH: 3 HOURS

■ **Tip:** Because the **Crock-Pot®** slow cooker cooks at a low heat for a long time, it's perfect for dishes calling for less-tender cuts of meat.

steak

- ¼ cup soy sauce
- 3 cloves garlic, minced
- 3 tablespoons honey
- 1 pound boneless beef chuck steak, about ¾ inch thick

dressing

- ¼ cup hoisin sauce
- 2 tablespoons creamy peanut butter
- ½ cup water
- 1 tablespoon minced fresh ginger
- 1 tablespoon ketchup *or* tomato paste
- 2 teaspoons lime juice
- 1 teaspoon sugar
- 2 cloves garlic, minced
- ¼ teaspoon hot chile sauce *or* sriracha*

salad

- ½ head savoy cabbage, shredded
- 1 bag (10 ounces) romaine lettuce with carrots and red cabbage
- 1 cup fresh cilantro leaves
- ½ cup chopped peanuts
- ¾ cup chopped mango
  Fresh lime wedges

Sriracha is a Thai hot sauce, also called "rooster sauce" because of the label on the bottle, and is available in Asian specialty markets.

1. Prepare steak: Coat 5- to 6-quart **Crock-Pot®** slow cooker with nonstick cooking spray. Combine soy sauce, garlic and honey in small bowl. Pour into **Crock-Pot®** slow cooker. Add steak, turning to coat. Cover; cook on HIGH 3 hours or until beef is tender.

2. Transfer beef to cutting board and let stand 10 minutes. Slice against the grain into ¼-inch strips. Cover with plastic wrap and refrigerate until needed.

3. Prepare dressing: Blend hoisin sauce and peanut butter until smooth. Add remaining dressing ingredients and mix until well blended.

4. Assemble salad: Toss cabbage and romaine salad mixture with dressing in large salad bowl. Top with reserved steak. Sprinkle with cilantro, peanuts and mango. Serve with lime wedge.

savory chicken and oregano chili

PREP TIME: 10 MINUTES

SERVINGS: 8

HIGH: 4 TO 5 HOURS

LOW: 8 TO 10 HOURS

■ **Tip:** Canned beans are ideal for **Crock-Pot®** slow cookers because they're already soft. Because salt, sugar and acidic ingredients can toughen dried beans as they cook, dried beans must be cooked and tender before you can add any of these other ingredients.

3 cans (15 ounces each) Great Northern or cannellini beans, drained
3½ cups chicken broth
2 cups chopped cooked chicken
2 medium red bell peppers, cored, seeded and chopped
1 medium onion, peeled and chopped
1 can (4 ounces) diced green chiles
3 cloves garlic, minced
2 teaspoons ground cumin
1 teaspoon salt
1 tablespoon minced fresh oregano

1. Place beans, broth, chicken, bell peppers, onion, chiles, garlic, cumin and salt in 5- to 6-quart **Crock-Pot®** slow cooker. Mix well to combine. Cover; cook on LOW 8 to 10 hours or on HIGH 4 to 5 hours.

2. Stir in oregano before serving.

jerk pork and sweet potato stew

PREP TIME: 15 MINUTES

SERVINGS: 4

LOW: 5 TO 6 HOURS

■ **Tip:** To reduce the amount of fat in **Crock-Pot®** slow cooker meals, trim excess fat from meats and degrease canned broth before adding.

2   tablespoons all-purpose flour
¼   teaspoon salt, or to taste
¼   teaspoon black pepper, or to taste
1¼ pounds pork shoulder, cut into bite-size pieces
2   tablespoons vegetable oil
1   large sweet potato, peeled and diced
1   cup frozen or canned corn
¼   cup minced green onions, green part only, divided
1   clove garlic, minced
½   medium scotch bonnet chile *or* jalapeño pepper,* cored, seeded and minced (about 1 teaspoon)
⅛   teaspoon ground allspice
1   cup chicken broth
1   tablespoon lime juice
2   cups cooked rice (optional)

*Scotch bonnet chiles and jalapeño peppers can sting and irritate the skin, so wear rubber gloves when handling and do not touch your eyes.

1. Combine flour, ¼ teaspoon salt and ¼ teaspoon pepper in resealable plastic food storage bag. Add pork and shake well to coat. Heat oil in large skillet over medium heat until hot. Add pork in a single layer (do in 2 batches, if necessary) and brown on both sides, about 5 minutes. Transfer to 4- or 5-quart **Crock-Pot®** slow cooker.

2. Add sweet potato, corn, 2 tablespoons green onions, garlic, chile and allspice. Stir in broth. Cover; cook on LOW 5 to 6 hours.

3. Stir in lime juice and remaining 2 tablespoons green onions. Adjust salt and pepper to taste. Serve stew over cooked rice, if desired.

cheesy shrimp on grits

PREP TIME: 15 MINUTES

SERVINGS: 6

HIGH: 2 HOURS,
20 MINUTES

LOW: 4 HOURS,
20 MINUTES

- 1 cup finely chopped green bell pepper
- 1 cup finely chopped red bell pepper
- ½ cup thinly sliced celery
- 1 bunch green onions, chopped, divided
- 4 tablespoons (½ stick) butter, cubed
- 1¼ teaspoons seafood seasoning
- 2 bay leaves
- ¼ teaspoon ground red pepper
- 1 pound uncooked shrimp, peeled, deveined and cleaned
- 5⅓ cups water
- 1⅓ cups quick-cooking grits
- 8 ounces shredded sharp Cheddar cheese
- ¼ cup whipping cream *or* half-and-half

1. Coat **Crock-Pot®** slow cooker with nonstick cooking spray. Add bell peppers, celery, all but ½ cup green onions, butter, seafood seasoning, bay leaves, and red pepper. Cover; cook on LOW 4 hours or on HIGH 2 hours.

2. Turn **Crock-Pot®** slow cooker to HIGH. Add shrimp. Cover; cook 15 minutes longer. Meanwhile, bring water to a boil in medium saucepan. Add grits and cook according to directions on package.

3. Discard bay leaves from shrimp mixture. Stir in cheese, cream, and remaining ½ cup green onions. Cook 5 minutes longer or until cheese has melted. Serve over grits.

■ **Variation:** This dish is also delicious served over polenta.

■ **Tip:** Seafood is delicate and should be added to the **Crock-Pot®** slow cooker during the last 15 to 30 minutes of the cooking time on the HIGH heat setting, and during the last 30 to 45 minutes on the LOW setting. Seafood overcooks easily, becoming tough and rubbery, so watch your cooking times, and cook only long enough for seafood to be done.

new mexican green chile pork stew

■ **Tip:** Root vegetables such as potatoes can sometimes take longer to cook in a **Crock-Pot®** slow cooker than meat. Place evenly cut vegetables on the bottom or along the sides of the **Crock-Pot®** slow cooker when possible.

1½ pounds boneless pork shoulder, cut into 1-inch cubes

2 medium baking potatoes *or* sweet potatoes, peeled and cut into large chunks

1 cup chopped onion

1 can (4 ounces) diced green chilies

1 cup frozen corn

2 teaspoons sugar

2 teaspoons cumin *or* chili powder

1 teaspoon dried oregano

1 jar (16 ounces) salsa verde (green salsa)

Hot cooked rice

¼ cup chopped fresh cilantro

1. Place pork, potatoes, onion, chilies and corn into 4-quart **Crock-Pot®** slow cooker. Stir sugar, cumin and oregano into salsa and pour over pork and vegetables. Stir gently to mix.

2. Cover; cook on LOW 6 to 8 hours or on HIGH 4 to 5 hours, or until pork is tender. Serve stew over hot rice and garnish with cilantro.

hearty lentil and root vegetable stew

2 cans (14½ ounces each) chicken broth
1 cup dried red lentils, rinsed and sorted
1½ cups turnips, cut into 1-inch cubes
1 medium onion, cut into ½-inch wedges
2 medium carrots, cut into 1-inch pieces
1 medium red bell pepper, cut into 1-inch pieces
½ teaspoon dried oregano
⅛ teaspoon red pepper flakes
1 tablespoon olive oil
½ teaspoon salt
4 slices bacon, crisp-cooked and crumbled
½ cup finely chopped green onions

1. Combine broth, lentils, turnips, onion, carrots, bell pepper, oregano and pepper flakes in **Crock-Pot®** slow cooker. Stir to mix well. Cover; cook on LOW 6 hours or on HIGH 3 hours, or until lentils are tender.

2. Stir in olive oil and salt. Sprinkle each serving with bacon and green onion.

PREP TIME: 15 MINUTES

SERVINGS: 8

HIGH: 3 HOURS

LOW: 6 HOURS

light meals

simply chili

PREP TIME: 15 MINUTES

SERVINGS: 6

LOW: 4 HOURS

3   **pounds 90% lean ground beef**

2   **cans (14½ ounces each) diced tomatoes, undrained**

2   **cans (14½ ounces each) chili beans, undrained**

2   **cups sliced onions**

1   **can (12 ounces) yellow corn, drained**

1   **cup chopped green bell pepper**

1   **can (8 ounces) tomato sauce**

3   **tablespoons chili powder**

1   **teaspoon garlic powder**

½   **teaspoon ground cumin**

½   **teaspoon dried oregano**

1. Heat large skillet over medium-high heat until hot. Add beef. Cook and stir until browned. Drain and discard excess fat. Transfer to 5-quart **Crock-Pot®** slow cooker.

2. Add tomatoes with juice, beans, onions, corn, bell pepper, tomato sauce, chili powder, garlic powder, cumin and oregano. Cover; cook on LOW 4 hours.

■ **Tip:** The flavor and aroma of crushed or ground herbs and spices may lessen during a longer cooking time. So, when slow cooking in your **Crock-Pot®** slow cooker, be sure to taste and adjust seasonings, if necessary, before serving.

lamb shanks and mushroom stew

PREP TIME: 20 MINUTES

SERVINGS: 4

HIGH: 4 TO 5 HOURS

LOW: 7 TO 8 HOURS

■ **Tip:** Recipes often provide a range of cooking times to account for variables, such as the altitude, the temperature of the ingredients before cooking or the quantity of food in your **Crock-Pot®** slow cooker. Always check for doneness before serving a dish.

2 tablespoons olive oil, divided
2 large lamb shanks (about 2 pounds total)
2 tablespoons all-purpose flour
2 cups sliced mushrooms*
1 small red onion, thinly sliced
1 large garlic clove, minced
1¼ cups chicken broth
½ cup pitted sliced green olives
¼ teaspoon salt, or to taste
⅛ teaspoon black pepper, or to taste
⅛ teaspoon crushed dried thyme
2 tablespoons capers
4 cups cooked noodles

Shiitake mushroom caps are preferred for this dish, but you may use other mushroom varieties, if necessary.

1. Heat 1 tablespoon oil in large skillet over medium-high heat until hot. Dust lamb shanks with flour, reserving leftover flour. Brown lamb on all sides, about 3 minutes per side. Transfer to 5- or 6-quart **Crock-Pot®** slow cooker.

2. Heat remaining 1 tablespoon oil in skillet over medium-high heat until hot. Add mushrooms, onion and garlic. Cook and stir 3 minutes or until vegetables are tender. Transfer mixture to **Crock-Pot®** slow cooker.

3. Sprinkle reserved flour into skillet and stir. Pour chicken broth into skillet. Stir to scrape up any browned bits. Continue to cook and stir 2 minutes longer or until mixture is slightly thickened. Pour into **Crock-Pot®** slow cooker.

4. Stir in olives, salt, pepper and thyme. Cover; cook on LOW 7 to 8 hours or on HIGH 4 to 5 hours.

5. Transfer lamb to cutting board. Gently pull lamb meat from bones with fork. Discard bones. Let cooking liquid stand 5 minutes. Skim off and discard excess fat. Return lamb to **Crock-Pot®** slow cooker. Stir in capers. Adjust seasoning, if desired. Serve lamb and sauce over noodles.

greek braised beef stew

PREP TIME: 15 MINUTES

SERVINGS: 6

HIGH: 6 TO 7 HOURS

■ **Tip:** Spinning or tapping the cover until the condensation falls off will allow you to see inside the **Crock-Pot®** slow cooker without removing the lid, which delays the cooking time.

¼ cup all-purpose flour
2 teaspoons Greek seasoning
¼ teaspoon salt, or to taste
¼ teaspoon black pepper, or to taste
2 pounds boneless beef stew meat or beef chuck roast, cut into 1-inch cubes
2 tablespoons olive oil
2 large onions, each cut into 8 wedges
1 container (10 ounces) grape or cherry tomatoes
1 jar (8 ounces) pitted kalamata olives, drained
8 sprigs fresh oregano, divided
1 lemon, divided
2 cups beef broth

1. Combine flour, Greek seasoning, salt and pepper in large resealable plastic food storage bag. Add beef, and shake to coat. Heat olive oil in large skillet over medium-high heat until hot. Add beef in single layer (do in 2 batches, if necessary) and brown on both sides, about 5 minutes. Transfer to **Crock-Pot®** slow cooker.

2. Add onions, tomatoes, olives, 4 sprigs oregano, juice of ½ lemon and broth. Cover; cook on HIGH 6 to 7 hours or until beef is tender. Add salt and pepper, if desired. Cut remaining ½ lemon into wedges and serve with stew. Garnish with remaining oregano.

main
dishes

main dishes

lemon pork chops

1 tablespoon vegetable oil
4 boneless pork chops
3 cans (8 ounces each) tomato sauce
1 large onion, quartered and sliced (optional)
1 large green bell pepper, cut into strips
1 tablespoon lemon-pepper seasoning
1 tablespoon Worcestershire sauce
1 large lemon, quartered
  Lemon wedges (optional)

1. Heat oil in large skillet over medium-low heat until hot. Brown pork chops on both sides. Drain and discard excess fat. Transfer to **Crock-Pot®** slow cooker.

2. Combine tomato sauce, onion, if desired, bell pepper, lemon-pepper seasoning and Worcestershire sauce. Add to **Crock-Pot®** slow cooker.

3. Squeeze juice from lemon quarters over mixture; drop squeezed lemon quarters into **Crock-Pot®** slow cooker. Cover; cook on LOW 6 to 8 hours or until pork is tender. Remove lemon wedges before serving. Garnish with additional lemon wedges, if desired.

PREP TIME: 15 MINUTES

SERVINGS: 4

LOW: 6 TO 8 HOURS

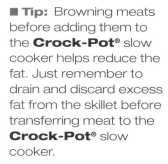

■ **Tip:** Browning meats before adding them to the **Crock-Pot®** slow cooker helps reduce the fat. Just remember to drain and discard excess fat from the skillet before transferring meat to the **Crock-Pot®** slow cooker.

main dishes
55

asian beef stew

PREP TIME: 10 MINUTES

SERVINGS: 6

HIGH: 5 HOURS, 20 MINUTES

2 onions, cut into ¼-inch slices
1½ pounds round steak, sliced thin across the grain
2 ribs celery, sliced
2 carrots, peeled and sliced *or* 1 cup peeled baby carrots
1 cup sliced mushrooms
1 cup orange juice
1 cup beef broth
⅓ cup hoisin sauce
2 tablespoons cornstarch
1 to 2 teaspoons Chinese five-spice powder *or* curry powder
1 cup frozen peas
 Hot cooked rice
 Chopped fresh cilantro (optional)

1. Place onions, beef, celery, carrots and mushrooms in 5-quart **Crock-Pot®** slow cooker.

2. Combine orange juice, broth, hoisin sauce, cornstarch and five-spice powder in small bowl. Pour into **Crock-Pot®** slow cooker. Cover; cook on HIGH 5 hours or until beef is tender.

3. Stir in peas. Cook 20 minutes longer or until peas are tender. Serve with hot cooked rice, and garnish with cilantro, if desired.

mango ginger pork roast

PREP TIME: 5 MINUTES

SERVINGS: 4 TO 6

LOW: 6 TO 8 HOURS, PLUS 3 TO 4 HOURS ON **HIGH**

1 pork shoulder roast (about 4 pounds)
½ to 1 teaspoon ground ginger, or to taste
 Salt and black pepper, to taste
2 cups mango salsa
2 tablespoons honey
¼ cup apricot preserves
 Hot cooked rice

1. Season roast with ginger, salt and pepper. Transfer to 4- to 6-quart **Crock-Pot®** slow cooker.

2. Combine salsa, honey and preserves. Pour over roast. Cover; cook on LOW 6 to 8 hours. Turn **Crock-Pot®** slow cooker to HIGH and cook 3 to 4 hours longer or until roast is tender. Serve over rice.

main dishes

asian beef stew

chicken marsala with fettuccine

■ **Tip:** Skinless chicken is usually best for recipes using the **Crock-Pot®** slow cooker, because the skin can shrivel and curl during cooking.

4   boneless, skinless chicken breasts
    Salt and black pepper, to taste
1   tablespoon vegetable oil
1   onion, chopped
½   cup Marsala wine
2   packages (6 ounces each) sliced brown mushrooms
½   cup chicken broth
2   teaspoons Worcestershire sauce
½   teaspoon salt
½   teaspoon freshly ground black pepper
½   cup whipping cream
2   tablespoons cornstarch
8   ounces cooked fettuccine
2   tablespoons chopped fresh parsley

1. Coat **Crock-Pot®** slow cooker with nonstick cooking spray. Season chicken with salt and pepper. Transfer to **Crock-Pot®** slow cooker.

2. Heat oil in large skillet over medium heat until hot. Add onion. Cook and stir until translucent. Add Marsala and continue cooking 2 to 3 minutes until mixture reduces slightly. Stir in mushrooms. Add broth, Worcestershire sauce, ½ teaspoon salt and ½ teaspoon pepper. Pour mixture over chicken. Cover; cook on HIGH 1½ to 1¾ hours or until chicken is done.

3. Transfer chicken to cutting board and let stand. Blend whipping cream and cornstarch until smooth. Stir into cooking liquid. Cover; cook 15 minutes longer or until mixture is thickened. Add salt and pepper, if desired.

4. Meanwhile, cook pasta according to directions on package. Drain and transfer to large serving bowl. Slice chicken breasts and place on pasta. Top with sauce and garnish with parsley.

main dishes

bistro chicken in rich cream sauce

PREP TIME: 5 MINUTES

SERVINGS: 4

HIGH: 3 HOURS, 15 MINUTES

LOW: 5 TO 6 HOURS

main dishes

4   bone-in chicken breast halves, rinsed and patted dry (about 3 pounds total)
½   cup dry white wine, divided
1   tablespoon *or* ½ packet (0.7 ounces) Italian salad dressing and seasoning mix
½   teaspoon dried oregano
1   can (10¾ ounces) cream of chicken soup
3   ounces cream cheese, cut into cubes
¼   teaspoon salt
⅛   teaspoon black pepper
2   tablespoons chopped fresh parsley

1. Coat 6-quart **Crock-Pot®** slow cooker with nonstick cooking spray. Arrange chicken in single layer in bottom, overlapping slightly. Pour ¼ cup wine over chicken. Sprinkle evenly with salad dressing mix and oregano. Cover; cook on LOW 5 to 6 hours or on HIGH 3 hours.

2. Transfer chicken to plate using slotted spoon. Turn **Crock-Pot®** slow cooker to HIGH. Whisk soup, cream cheese, salt and pepper into cooking liquid. (Mixture will be a bit lumpy.) Arrange chicken on top. Cover; cook 15 to 20 minutes longer to heat through.

3. Transfer chicken to shallow pasta bowl. Add remaining ¼ cup wine to sauce and whisk until smooth. To serve, spoon sauce around chicken, and garnish with parsley.

chicken in honey sauce

PREP TIME: 5 MINUTES

SERVINGS: 6

HIGH: 3 TO 4 HOURS

LOW: 6 TO 8 HOURS

6   boneless, skinless chicken breasts (about 1½ pounds)
     Salt and black pepper, to taste
2   cups honey
1   cup soy sauce
½   cup ketchup
¼   cup oil
2   cloves garlic, minced
     Sesame seeds, for garnish

1. Place chicken in **Crock-Pot®** slow cooker; season with salt and pepper.

2. Combine honey, soy sauce, ketchup, oil and garlic in medium bowl. Pour over chicken. Cover; cook on LOW 6 to 8 hours or on HIGH 3 to 4 hours.

3. Garnish with sesame seeds before serving. Serve extra sauce on side, if desired.

spicy turkey
with citrus au jus

1   bone-in turkey breast,
    thawed, rinsed and
    patted dry (about
    4 pounds)
4   tablespoons (½ stick)
    butter, at room
    temperature
    Grated peel of 1 medium
    lemon
1   teaspoon chili powder
¼   to ½ teaspoon coarsely
    ground black pepper
⅛   to ¼ teaspoon red
    pepper flakes
1   tablespoon lemon juice
    Salt and black pepper, to
    taste

1. Coat **Crock-Pot®** slow cooker with nonstick cooking spray. Add turkey breast.

2. Mix butter, lemon peel, chili powder, black pepper and pepper flakes in small bowl until well blended. Spread mixture over top and sides of turkey. Cover; cook on LOW 4 to 6 hours or on HIGH 3 to 4 hours, or until tender.

3. Transfer turkey to cutting board. Let stand 10 minutes before slicing. Turn **Crock-Pot®** slow cooker to LOW.

4. Stir lemon juice into cooking liquid. Pour mixture through fine-mesh sieve; discard solids in sieve. Let mixture stand 5 minutes. Skim and discard excess fat. Add salt and pepper, if desired. Return au jus mixture to **Crock-Pot®** slow cooker and cover to keep warm. Serve au jus with turkey.

PREP TIME: 10 MINUTES

SERVINGS: 6 TO 8

HIGH: 3 TO 4 HOURS

LOW: 4 TO 6 HOURS

■ **Tip:** To remove fat from the cooking liquid of cooked **Crock-Pot®** slow cooker dishes, first remove any solid foods from the cooking liquid. Let the cooking liquid stand 5 minutes to allow the fat to rise to the surface, then skim off the fat with a large spoon.

main dishes

61

autumn apricot beef ragoût

PREP TIME: 10 MINUTES

SERVINGS: 3 TO 4

LOW: 8 TO 10 HOURS

■ **Tip:** For the best results, always fill your **Crock-Pot®** slow cooker one-half to three-quarters full of ingredients.

1 **pound boneless beef round steak, cut into bite-size pieces**
⅔ **cup apricot nectar**
1 **cup medium thick-and-chunky salsa**
1 **teaspoon ground pumpkin pie spice**
¼ **teaspoon salt**
½ **cup chopped dried apricots**
½ **cup green onions, sliced**
3 **tablespoons water**
2 **tablespoons all-purpose flour**
3 **cups hot cooked rice**
¼ **cup chopped fresh cilantro**

1. Place beef, nectar, salsa, pumpkin pie spice and salt in 3-quart **Crock-Pot®** slow cooker. Cover; cook on LOW 8 to 10 hours.

2. Turn **Crock-Pot®** slow cooker to HIGH. Add apricots and green onions. Cover; cook 10 minutes longer.

3. Stir water and flour in small bowl until smooth. Add to **Crock-Pot®** slow cooker and stir well to combine. Cover; cook on HIGH 15 minutes or until thickened.

4. Serve ragoût over rice. Garnish with cilantro.

rosemary pork
with red wine risotto

PREP TIME: 15 MINUTES

SERVINGS: 4 TO 6

HIGH: 3 TO 5 HOURS

■ **Tip:** The flavor and aroma of crushed or ground herbs and spices may lessen during a longer cooking time. Whole herbs and spices hold up better for all-day cooking. Be sure to taste and adjust your seasonings before serving.

1   **boneless pork loin (about 3 pounds)**
1   **teaspoon salt**
1   **teaspoon black pepper**
2   **tablespoons olive oil**
6   **sprigs fresh rosemary, divided**
2   **cups chicken broth, divided**
2   **tablespoons butter, divided**
3   **cloves garlic, minced**
½   **cup minced onion**
1   **cup arborio rice**
1   **cup fruity red wine**
¾   **cup grated Parmesan cheese**

1. Season pork with salt and pepper. Heat oil in large skillet over medium-high heat until hot. Add 3 sprigs of rosemary and place pork roast on top. Brown pork roast on all sides, about 5 to 7 minutes. Transfer roast and rosemary to **Crock-Pot®** slow cooker.

2. Add ¼ cup broth to skillet. Cook and stir, loosening browned bits. Add 1 tablespoon butter, garlic and onion. Cook and stir until onion is translucent.

3. Add rice to skillet. Cook and stir until rice just begins to brown, about 2 minutes. Stir in wine and remaining 1¾ cups broth. Pour mixture around roast. Cover; cook on HIGH 3 to 5 hours, stirring occasionally, until roast is tender.

4. Remove and discard rosemary. Transfer roast to serving platter. Let stand 10 minutes before slicing.

5. Stir remaining 1 tablespoon butter and Parmesan cheese into rice. Serve risotto with roast and garnish with remaining rosemary.

brisket with bacon, bleu cheese & onions

PREP TIME: 15 MINUTES

SERVINGS: 6 TO 8

HIGH: 5 TO 7 HOURS

■ **Tip:** Use freshly ground pepper as a quick and simple flavor enhancer for **Crock-Pot®** slow cooker dishes.

2   large sweet* onions, sliced into ½-inch rounds
6   slices bacon
1   flat-cut boneless beef brisket (about 3½ pounds)
    Salt and black pepper, to taste
2   cans (10½ ounces each) condensed beef consommé, undiluted
1   teaspoon cracked black peppercorns
3   ounces crumbled bleu cheese

Maui, Vidalia or Walla Walla onions are preferred.

1. Coat 5- to 6-quart **Crock-Pot®** slow cooker with nonstick cooking spray. Line bottom with onion slices.

2. Heat large skillet over medium-high heat until hot. Add bacon and cook only until chewy, not crisp. Remove from skillet using slotted spoon. Drain on paper towels, and chop.

3. Season brisket with salt and pepper. Place in skillet. Sear brisket in bacon fat on all sides, turning as it browns. Transfer to **Crock-Pot®** slow cooker.

4. Pour in consommé. Sprinkle brisket with peppercorns and half of reserved bacon. Cover; cook on HIGH 5 to 7 hours or until meat is tender.

5. Transfer brisket to cutting board and let stand 10 minutes. Slice against the grain into ¾-inch slices. To serve, arrange onions on serving platter and spread slices of brisket on top. Sprinkle on bleu cheese and remaining bacon. Add salt and pepper to cooking liquid, if desired, and serve with brisket.

mediterranean pepper pot

1 pound mild Italian sausage, removed from casings

1½ cups water

1 can (15 ounces) navy beans, rinsed and drained

¼ cup chopped pepperoncini peppers*

1 medium yellow bell pepper, cut into 1-inch pieces

1 medium green bell pepper, cut into 1-inch pieces

1 can (14½ ounces) diced canned tomatoes

2 teaspoons dried basil

1 teaspoon dried oregano

¼ cup ketchup

*Pepperoncini are pickled peppers sold in jars with brine. They're available in the supermarket condiment aisle.

1. Coat **Crock-Pot®** slow cooker with nonstick cooking spray. Heat large skillet over medium-high heat until hot. Add sausage and brown well. Drain and discard excess fat. Transfer to **Crock-Pot®** slow cooker.

2. Add water, beans, peppers, tomatoes with juice, basil and oregano. Cover; cook on LOW 7 to 8 hours or on HIGH 3 to 4 hours.

3. Add ketchup; stir well. Let stand, covered, 15 minutes before serving.

PREP TIME: 15 MINUTES

SERVINGS: 4

HIGH: 3 TO 4 HOURS

LOW: 7 TO 8 HOURS

■ **Tip:** For instant flavor, serve entrées and main dishes made in your **Crock-Pot®** slow cooker with a garnish of freshly grated cheese, such as Parmesan, Romano or Asiago.

main dishes

cuban-style curried turkey

PREP TIME: 15 MINUTES

SERVINGS: 8

LOW: 1 HOUR

■ **Tip:** Curry powder is a blend of different spices and can vary in spiciness from mild to quite hot. If you prefer a hotter flavor, look for Madras curry powder.

4 tablespoons all-purpose flour

1 teaspoon salt, or to taste

½ teaspoon black pepper, or to taste

2 pounds turkey breast meat,* cut into 1-inch cubes

4 tablespoons vegetable oil, divided

2 small onions, chopped

2 garlic cloves, minced

2 cans (14½ ounces each) diced tomatoes, undrained

2 cans (15 ounces each) black beans, rinsed and drained

1 cup chicken broth

⅔ cup raisins

½ teaspoon curry powder

¼ teaspoon crushed red pepper flakes

Juice of 1 lime (2 tablespoons)

2 tablespoons minced fresh cilantro

2 tablespoons minced green onion, green part only

4 cups cooked rice (optional)

You may substitute turkey tenderloins, cut as directed.

1. Combine flour, salt and pepper in resealable plastic food storage bag. Add turkey cubes and shake well to coat. Heat 2 tablespoons oil in large skillet over medium heat until hot. Add turkey and brown on all sides in batches, about 5 minutes per batch. Transfer to 5- to 6-quart **Crock-Pot®** slow cooker.

2. Heat remaining 2 tablespoons oil in skillet. Add onions and cook and stir over medium heat 3 minutes or until golden. Stir in garlic and cook an additional 30 seconds. Transfer to **Crock-Pot®** slow cooker.

3. Stir in tomatoes with juice, beans, broth, raisins, curry powder and red pepper flakes. Cover; cook on LOW 1 hour. Stir in lime juice. Sprinkle with cilantro and green onion. Adjust seasonings, if desired. Serve over rice, if desired.

spicy citrus pork with pineapple salsa

PREP TIME: 15 MINUTES

SERVINGS: 12

HIGH: 1 HOUR,
10 MINUTES

LOW: 2 TO 2¼ HOURS

■ **Tip:** If your pepper mill doesn't produce a coarse grind, you can place whole peppercorns in a plastic bag and use a rolling pin to crush and grind them neatly.

1   tablespoon ground cumin
½   teaspoon salt
1   teaspoon coarsely ground black pepper
3   pounds center-cut pork loin, rinsed and patted dry
2   tablespoons vegetable oil
4   cans (8 ounces each) pineapple tidbits* in own juice, drained, ½ cup juice reserved
4   tablespoons lemon juice, divided
2   teaspoons grated lemon peel
1   cup finely chopped orange or red bell pepper
4   tablespoons finely chopped red onion
2   tablespoons chopped fresh cilantro *or* mint
1   teaspoon grated fresh ginger (optional)
¼   teaspoon red pepper flakes (optional)

*If tidbits are unavailable, purchase pineapple chunks, and coarsely chop.

1. Coat **Crock-Pot®** slow cooker with nonstick cooking spray. Combine cumin, salt and pepper in small bowl. Rub evenly onto pork. Heat oil in medium skillet over medium-high heat until hot. Sear pork loin on all sides, turning as it browns, 1 to 2 minutes per side. Transfer to **Crock-Pot®** slow cooker.

2. Spoon 4 tablespoons of reserved pineapple juice and 2 tablespoons lemon juice over pork. Cover; cook on LOW 2 to 2¼ hours or on HIGH 1 hour and 10 minutes, or until meat is tender.

3. Prepare salsa: Combine pineapple, remaining 2 tablespoons pineapple juice, remaining 1 tablespoon lemon juice, lemon peel, bell pepper, onion, cilantro, ginger, if desired, and pepper flakes, if desired, in medium bowl. Toss gently and blend well; set aside.

4. Transfer pork to serving platter. Let pork stand 10 minutes before slicing. Arrange pork slices on serving platter. To serve, pour sauce evenly over slices. Serve salsa on side.

ham with fruited bourbon sauce

PREP TIME: 5 MINUTES

SERVINGS: 10 TO 12

HIGH: 4½ TO 5 HOURS

LOW: 9 TO 10 HOURS

■ **Tip:** For easier cleanup of the **Crock-Pot®** slow cooker stoneware, spray the inside with nonstick cooking spray before adding ingredients.

1   **bone-in ham, butt portion (about 6 pounds)**
½   **cup apple juice**
¾   **cup packed dark brown sugar**
½   **cup raisins**
1   **teaspoon ground cinnamon**
¼   **teaspoon red pepper flakes**
⅓   **cup dried cherries**
¼   **cup cornstarch**
¼   **cup bourbon, rum *or* apple juice**

1. Coat 5-quart **Crock-Pot®** slow cooker with nonstick cooking spray. Add ham, cut side up. Combine apple juice, brown sugar, raisins, cinnamon and pepper flakes in small bowl; stir well. Pour mixture evenly over ham. Cover; cook on LOW 9 to 10 hours or on HIGH 4½ to 5 hours. Add cherries 30 minutes before end of cooking time.

2. Transfer ham to cutting board. Let stand 15 minutes before slicing.

3. Pour cooking liquid into large measuring cup and let stand 5 minutes. Skim and discard excess fat. Return cooking liquid to **Crock-Pot®** slow cooker.

4. Turn **Crock-Pot®** slow cooker to HIGH. Whisk cornstarch and bourbon in small bowl until cornstarch is dissolved. Stir into cooking liquid. Cover; cook 15 to 20 minutes longer or until thickened. Serve sauce over sliced ham.

main dishes

jalapeño brisket

PREP TIME: 10 MINUTES

SERVINGS: 8 TO 10

LOW: 8 TO 9 HOURS

2   onions, sliced
1   beef brisket, trimmed of excess fat (about 5 to 6 pounds)
2   tablespoons soy sauce
1   tablespoon minced garlic
2   tablespoons cornstarch
1   can (15 ounces) tomato sauce
1   jar (about 11½ ounces) sliced mild jalapeño peppers,* undrained
    Chopped fresh cilantro, for garnish
    Sour cream (optional)

*Jalapeño nacho slices are available in both mild and hot varieties. If using sliced hot jalapeño peppers, use ½ jar.

1. Place onions in 6-quart **Crock-Pot®** slow cooker. Rub all sides of brisket with soy sauce. Sprinkle garlic over brisket and place on onions, fat side up.

2. Stir cornstarch into tomato sauce and pour over brisket. Sprinkle jalapeño slices on top, and add any liquid from jar. Cover; cook on LOW 8 to 9 hours or until brisket is tender.

3. Transfer brisket to serving platter. Skim and discard excess fat from sauce. To serve, slice brisket thinly against the grain and spoon on warm sauce.

lemon and herb turkey breast

PREP TIME: 10 MINUTES

SERVINGS: 6

HIGH: 4 TO 5 HOURS

LOW: 8 TO 10 HOURS

1   split turkey breast (about 3 pounds)
½   cup lemon juice
6   cloves garlic, minced
¼   teaspoon dried parsley
¼   teaspoon dried tarragon
¼   teaspoon dried rosemary
¼   teaspoon dried sage
¼   teaspoon salt
¼   teaspoon black pepper
½   cup dry white wine

1. Place turkey breast in 5- to 6-quart **Crock-Pot®** slow cooker, adjusting turkey to fit as needed.

2. Combine remaining ingredients in small bowl. Pour over turkey breast. Cover; cook on LOW 8 to 10 hours or on HIGH 4 to 5 hours.

3. Transfer turkey to serving platter. Let stand 10 minutes before slicing to serve.

chicken provençal

2 pounds boneless, skinless chicken thighs, each cut into quarters

2 medium red bell peppers, cut into ¼-inch thick slices

1 medium yellow bell pepper, cut into ¼-inch thick slices

1 onion, thinly sliced

1 can (28 ounces) plum tomatoes, drained

3 cloves garlic, minced

¼ teaspoon salt

¼ teaspoon thyme

¼ teaspoon fennel seeds, crushed

3 strips orange peel

½ cup chopped fresh basil

1. Place chicken, bell peppers, onion, tomatoes, garlic, salt, thyme, fennel seeds and orange peel in **Crock-Pot®** slow cooker. Stir to mix well. Cover; cook on LOW 7 to 9 hours or on HIGH 3 to 4 hours, or until chicken is tender.

2. Garnish with basil before serving.

PREP TIME: 15 MINUTES

SERVINGS: 8

HIGH: 3 TO 4 HOURS

LOW: 7 TO 9 HOURS

■ **Tip:** Add more color and variety to this dish by using green or orange bell peppers, if desired.

greek chicken and orzo

PREP TIME: 5 MINUTES

SERVINGS: 4

HIGH: 3 TO 4 HOURS

LOW: 5 TO 6 HOURS

■ **Tip:** Browning skin-on chicken not only adds flavor and color, but also prevents the skin from shrinking and curling during the long, slow cooking process.

2   medium green bell peppers, cut into thin strips
1   cup chopped onion
2   teaspoons extra-virgin olive oil
8   chicken thighs, rinsed and patted dry
1   tablespoon dried oregano
½   teaspoon dried rosemary
½   teaspoon garlic powder
¾   teaspoon salt, divided
⅜   teaspoon black pepper, divided
8   ounces uncooked dry orzo pasta
     Juice and grated peel of 1 medium lemon
½   cup water
2   ounces crumbled feta cheese (optional)
     Chopped fresh parsley (optional)

1. Coat 6-quart **Crock-Pot®** slow cooker with nonstick cooking spray. Add bell peppers and onion.

2. Heat oil in large skillet over medium-high heat until hot. Brown chicken on both sides. Transfer to **Crock-Pot®** slow cooker, overlapping slightly if necessary. Sprinkle chicken with oregano, rosemary, garlic powder, ¼ teaspoon salt and ⅛ teaspoon black pepper. Cover; cook on LOW 5 to 6 hours or on HIGH 3 to 4 hours, or until chicken is tender.

3. Transfer chicken to separate plate. Turn **Crock-Pot®** slow cooker to HIGH. Stir orzo, lemon juice, lemon peel, water, and remaining ½ teaspoon salt and ¼ teaspoon black pepper into **Crock-Pot®** slow cooker. Top with chicken. Cover; cook 30 minutes or until pasta is done. Garnish with feta cheese and parsley, if desired.

asian ginger beef over bok choy

PREP TIME: 15 MINUTES

SERVINGS: 6 TO 8

HIGH: 3 TO 4 HOURS

LOW: 7 TO 8 HOURS

■ **Tip:** Use your **Crock-Pot®** slow cooker to make large batches. Freeze leftovers in individual portions. Just reheat a single serving in the microwave for fast meals or impulse snacks.

2 tablespoons peanut oil
1½ pounds boneless beef chuck roast, cut into 1-inch pieces
3 green onions, cut into ½-inch slices
6 cloves garlic
1 cup chicken broth
½ cup water
¼ cup soy sauce
2 teaspoons ground ginger
1 teaspoon Asian chili paste
9 ounces fresh udon noodles *or* vermicelli, cooked and drained
3 cups bok choy, trimmed, washed and cut into 1-inch pieces
½ cup minced fresh cilantro

1. Heat oil in large skillet over medium-high heat until hot. Sear beef on all sides in batches to prevent crowding, turning each piece as it browns. Sear last batch of beef with onions and garlic.

2. Transfer to 5- to 6-quart **Crock-Pot®** slow cooker. Add broth, water, soy sauce, ginger and chili paste. Stir well to combine. Cover; cook on LOW 7 to 8 hours or on HIGH 3 to 4 hours, or until beef is very tender.

3. Just before serving, turn **Crock-Pot®** slow cooker to HIGH. Add noodles and stir well. Add bok choy and stir again. Heat on HIGH until bok choy is tender-crisp, about 15 minutes.

4. Garnish beef with cilantro and serve while hot.

turkey scaloppine in alfredo sauce

PREP TIME: 10 MINUTES

SERVINGS: 4

LOW: 1 TO 1½ HOURS

2   tablespoons all-purpose flour
¼   teaspoon salt, or to taste
¼   teaspoon black pepper
1   pound turkey tenderloins, cut lengthwise in half
1   tablespoon butter
1   tablespoon olive oil
1   cup refrigerated Alfredo pasta sauce
12 ounces spinach noodles
¼   cup shredded Asiago or Parmesan cheese

1. Place flour, salt and pepper in resealable plastic storage bag. Add turkey and shake well to coat. Heat butter and oil in large skillet over medium-high heat until hot. Add turkey in single layer. Brown on all sides, about 3 minutes per side. Arrange turkey in single layer in **Crock-Pot®** slow cooker.

2. Add Alfredo sauce. Cover; cook on LOW 1 to 1½ hours or until turkey is tender.

3. Meanwhile, cook noodles until tender. Drain and place in large shallow bowl. Spoon turkey and sauce over noodles. Garnish with cheese.

golden pork with cinnamon-sugar apples

PREP TIME: 5 MINUTES

SERVINGS: 6

LOW: 9 HOURS

1   pork loin roast (about 3 pounds)
1   can condensed golden mushroom soup, undiluted
½   cup water
¼   cup packed brown sugar
2   tablespoons soy sauce
¼   cup granulated sugar
3   tablespoons ground cinnamon
2   Granny Smith apples, cored and sliced
    Hot cooked rice or noodles

1. Place pork in **Crock-Pot®** slow cooker.

2. Combine soup, water, brown sugar and soy sauce in medium bowl; stir to mix well. Pour over pork. Cover; cook on LOW 8 hours.

3. About 1 hour before serving, combine granulated sugar and cinnamon in medium resealable plastic food storage bag. Add apples; shake to coat well. Place apples on top of pork. Cover; cook 1 hour longer. Serve with rice or noodles.

80

turkey paprikash

2 tablespoons all-purpose flour

¼ teaspoon salt, or to taste

¼ teaspoon black pepper, or to taste

¼ teaspoon sweet paprika

⅛ teaspoon crushed red pepper flakes

1 pound turkey tenderloins, cut lengthwise in half

2 tablespoons olive oil

1 small onion, chopped

1 garlic clove, minced

1 can (14½ ounces) diced tomatoes, undrained

12 ounces noodles

¼ cup sour cream

¼ cup pitted sliced green olives

1. Place flour, salt, pepper, paprika and pepper flakes in resealable plastic food storage bag. Add turkey and shake well to coat. Heat oil in large skillet over medium-high heat until hot. Add turkey in single layer. Brown on all sides, about 3 minutes per side. Arrange turkey in single layer in **Crock-Pot®** slow cooker.

2. Add onion and garlic to skillet. Cook and stir over medium-high heat 2 minutes or until onion begins to turn golden. Transfer to **Crock-Pot®** slow cooker. Stir in tomatoes with juice. Cover; cook on LOW 1 to 2 hours or until turkey is tender.

3. Meanwhile, cook noodles until tender. Drain and place in large shallow bowl. Spoon turkey and sauce over noodles. Top with sour cream and olives.

■ **Tip:** Don't add water to the **Crock-Pot®** slow cooker unless the recipe specifically says to do so. Foods don't lose as much moisture during slow cooking as they do during conventional cooking, so follow recipe guidelines for best results.

main dishes

chicken and artichoke-parmesan dressing

PREP TIME: 5 MINUTES

SERVINGS: 6

HIGH: 3 HOURS,
20 MINUTES

■ **Tip:** Ground paprika helps to lend color, as well as flavor, to poultry, eliminating the need to brown the meat first.

2 cans (14 ounces each) quartered artichoke hearts, drained and coarsely chopped
4 ounces herb-seasoned stuffing
1½ cups frozen seasoning-blend* vegetables, thawed
¾ cup mayonnaise
¾ cup grated Parmesan cheese, divided
1 large egg, beaten
½ teaspoon paprika
½ teaspoon dried oregano
½ teaspoon salt
¼ teaspoon black pepper
6 bone-in chicken breast halves, rinsed and patted dry (about 3½ pounds)
Grated Parmesan cheese, for garnish

Seasoning-blend vegetables are a mixture of chopped bell peppers, onions and celery. If you're unable to find frozen vegetables, use ½ cup of each fresh vegetable.

1. Coat 6-quart **Crock-Pot®** slow cooker with cooking spray. Combine artichokes, stuffing, vegetables, mayonnaise, all but 1 tablespoon Parmesan and egg in large bowl. Stir gently and blend well. Transfer mixture to **Crock-Pot®** slow cooker.

2. Combine paprika, oregano, salt and pepper in small bowl. Rub evenly onto chicken. Arrange chicken on artichoke mixture in **Crock-Pot®** slow cooker, overlapping slightly. Cover; cook on HIGH 3 hours.

3. Transfer chicken to serving platter. Cover with foil to keep warm. Stir artichoke mixture in **Crock-Pot®** slow cooker. Sprinkle evenly with remaining 1 tablespoon Parmesan. Cook, uncovered, 20 to 25 minutes or until thickened. Serve dressing with chicken.

hearty cassoulet

PREP TIME: 15 MINUTES

SERVINGS: 6

LOW: 4 TO 4½ HOURS

■ **Tip:** For easier meal preparation, cut up ingredients for a **Crock-Pot®** slow cooker recipe the night before.

1 tablespoon olive oil

1 large onion, finely chopped

4 boneless, skinless chicken thighs (about 1 pound), chopped

¼ pound smoked turkey sausage, finely chopped

3 cloves garlic, minced

1 teaspoon dried thyme

½ teaspoon black pepper

4 tablespoons tomato paste

2 tablespoons water

3 cans (about 15 ounces each) Great Northern beans, rinsed and drained

½ cup dry bread crumbs

3 tablespoons minced fresh parsley

1. Heat oil in large skillet over medium heat until hot. Add onion; cook and stir 5 minutes or until onion is tender. Stir in chicken, sausage, garlic, thyme and pepper. Cook 5 minutes or until chicken and sausage are browned.

2. Remove skillet from heat; stir in tomato paste and water until blended. Place beans and chicken mixture in **Crock-Pot®** slow cooker. Cover; cook on LOW 4 to 4½ hours or until meat is tender.

3. Before serving, combine bread crumbs and parsley in small bowl. Sprinkle over cassoulet.

soups
&sides

cioppino

1 pound cod, halibut or any firm-fleshed white fish, cubed
1 cup mushrooms, sliced
2 carrots, sliced
1 onion, chopped
1 green bell pepper, chopped
1 teaspoon minced garlic
1 can (15 ounces) tomato sauce
1 can (14 ounces) beef broth
1 teaspoon salt
½ teaspoon black pepper
½ teaspoon dried oregano
1 can (7 ounces) cooked clams
½ pound cooked shrimp
1 package (6 ounces) cooked crabmeat
  Minced parsley

1. Combine fish, mushrooms, carrots, onion, bell pepper, garlic, tomato sauce, broth, salt, black pepper and oregano in **Crock-Pot®** slow cooker. Cover; cook on LOW 10 to 12 hours.

2. Turn **Crock-Pot®** slow cooker to HIGH. Add clams, shrimp and crabmeat. Cover; cook 15 to 30 minutes or until seafood is heated through. Garnish with parsley before serving.

PREP TIME: 20 TO 30 MINUTES

SERVINGS: 6

LOW: 10 TO 12½ HOURS

soups & sides

hearty chicken tequila soup

PREP TIME: 10 MINUTES

SERVINGS: 2 TO 4

LOW: 8 TO 10 HOURS

■ **Tip:** Defrost meat and vegetables before cooking them in the **Crock-Pot®** slow cooker.

1   small onion, cut into 8 wedges
1   cup frozen corn, thawed
1   can (14½ ounces) diced tomatoes with mild green chilies, undrained
2   cloves garlic, minced
2   tablespoons chopped fresh cilantro, plus additional for garnish
1   whole fryer chicken (about 3½ pounds)
2   cups chicken broth
3   tablespoons tequila
¼   cup sour cream

1. Spread onions on bottom of **Crock-Pot®** slow cooker. Add corn, tomatoes, garlic and 2 tablespoons cilantro. Mix well to combine. Place chicken on top of tomato mixture.

2. Combine broth and tequila in medium bowl. Pour over chicken and tomato mixture. Cover; cook on LOW 8 to 10 hours.

3. Transfer chicken to cutting board. Remove skin and bones. Pull meat apart with 2 forks into bite-size pieces. Return chicken to **Crock-Pot®** slow cooker and stir.

4. Serve with dollop of sour cream and garnish with cilantro.

soups & sides

italian hillside garden soup

PREP TIME: 15 MINUTES

SERVINGS: 6

HIGH: 4 HOURS

LOW: 7 HOURS

■ **Tip:** Cooking times are guidelines. **Crock-Pot®** slow cookers, just like ovens, cook differently depending on a variety of factors, including capacity. For example, cooking times will be longer at higher altitudes.

1 tablespoon extra-virgin olive oil
1 cup chopped green bell pepper
1 cup chopped onion
½ cup sliced celery
1 can (14½ ounces) diced tomatoes with basil, garlic and oregano, undrained
1 can (15½ ounces) navy beans, rinsed and drained
1 medium zucchini, chopped
1 cup frozen cut green beans, thawed
2 cans (14 ounces each) chicken broth
¼ teaspoon garlic powder
1 package (9 ounces) refrigerated sausage- or cheese-filled tortellini pasta
3 tablespoons chopped fresh basil
Grated Asiago or Parmesan cheese

1. Heat oil in large skillet over medium-high heat until hot. Add bell pepper, onion and celery. Cook and stir 4 minutes or until onions are translucent. Transfer to 5-quart **Crock-Pot®** slow cooker.

2. Add tomatoes with juice, navy beans, zucchini, green beans, broth and garlic powder. Cover; cook on LOW 7 hours or on HIGH 3½ hours.

3. Turn **Crock-Pot®** slow cooker to HIGH. Add tortellini and cook 20 to 25 minutes longer or until pasta is tender. Stir in basil. Garnish each serving with cheese.

soups & sides

fresh lime and black bean soup

PREP TIME: 10 MINUTES

SERVINGS: 4

HIGH: 3½ HOURS

LOW: 7 HOURS

2	cans (15 ounces each) black beans, undrained
1	can (14 ounces) reduced-sodium chicken broth
1½	cups chopped onion
1½	teaspoons chili powder
¾	teaspoon ground cumin
¼	teaspoon garlic powder
⅛	to ¼ teaspoon red pepper flakes
½	cup sour cream
2	tablespoons extra-virgin olive oil
2	tablespoons chopped cilantro
1	medium lime, cut into wedges

1. Coat 3- to 4-quart **Crock-Pot®** slow cooker with nonstick cooking spray. Add beans, broth, onions, chili powder, cumin, garlic powder and pepper flakes. Cover; cook on LOW 7 hours or on HIGH 3½ hours, or until onions are very soft.

2. Process 1 cup of soup mixture in blender until smooth and return to **Crock-Pot®** slow cooker. Stir and repeat with additional 1 cup mixture. Let stand 15 to 20 minutes before serving.

3. Ladle soup into 4 bowls. Divide sour cream, oil and cilantro evenly among servings. Squeeze juice from lime wedge over each.

■ **Tip:** Brighten the flavor of dishes cooked in the **Crock-Pot®** slow cooker by adding fresh herbs or fresh lemon or lime juice before serving.

soups & sides

potato and spinach soup with gouda

9 medium Yukon Gold potatoes, peeled and cubed (about 6 cups)

2 cans (14 ounces each) chicken broth

½ cup water

1 small red onion, finely chopped

5 ounces baby spinach

½ teaspoon salt

¼ teaspoon ground red pepper

¼ teaspoon black pepper

2½ cups shredded smoked Gouda cheese, divided

1 can (12 ounces) evaporated milk

1 tablespoon olive oil

4 cloves garlic, cut into thin slices

5 to 7 sprigs parsley, finely chopped

1. Combine potatoes, broth, water, onion, spinach, salt and red and black pepper in **Crock-Pot®** slow cooker. Cover; cook on LOW 10 hours or on HIGH 4 to 5 hours, or until potatoes are tender.

2. Turn **Crock-Pot®** slow cooker to HIGH. Slightly mash potatoes in **Crock-Pot®** slow cooker. Add 2 cups Gouda and evaporated milk; stir to mix well. Cover; cook on HIGH 15 to 20 minutes or until cheese melts.

3. Heat oil in small skillet over low heat until hot. Cook and stir garlic until golden brown; set aside. Pour soup into bowls. Top each bowl with 2 to 3 teaspoons remaining Gouda. Place spoonful of garlic in center of each bowl; sprinkle with parsley.

PREP TIME: 10 MINUTES

SERVINGS: 8 TO 10

HIGH: 4 TO 5 HOURS

LOW: 10 HOURS

soups & sides

91

red bean soup with andouille sausage

PREP TIME: 1 HOUR
(FOR BEANS)

SERVINGS: 6 TO 8

HIGH: 4½ HOURS

■ **Tip:** You may substitute canned beans for the dried beans in this recipe. Canned beans are ideal for **Crock-Pot®** slow cookers because they're already soft. Because salt, sugar and acidic ingredients can toughen dried beans as they cook, the cooking times can be longer for recipes using dried beans.

1½ cups dried red kidney beans, soaked in cold water 1 hour, drained and rinsed
2 tablespoons unsalted butter
1 large sweet onion, diced
3 stalks celery, diced
2 large cloves garlic, chopped
8 cups chicken broth
1 ham hock
1 bay leaf
2 parsnips, diced
1 sweet potato, peeled and diced
1 pound andouille sausage *or* kielbasa, cut into ½-inch pieces.
Salt and black pepper, to taste

1. Soak beans in cold water 1 hour. Drain and rinse.

2. Meanwhile, melt butter in large saucepan over medium heat. Add onion, celery and garlic. Cook and stir 5 minutes or until onions are translucent. Transfer to 5- or 6-quart **Crock-Pot®** slow cooker.

3. Add beans, broth, ham and bay leaf. Cover; cook on HIGH 2 hours.

4. Remove and discard ham hock. Add parsnips and sweet potato. Cover; cook on HIGH 2 hours.

5. Add sausage. Cover; cook 30 minutes longer or until heated through. Remove and discard bay leaf before serving. Add salt and pepper, if desired.

92

golden potato-cheese soup

1 tablespoon butter
1 large onion, chopped
1 clove garlic, sliced
5 cups whole milk
2 pounds Yukon Gold
   potatoes, scrubbed
   and diced
1/8 teaspoon ground red
   pepper
2 cups (8 ounces)
   shredded extra-sharp
   Cheddar cheese
1 teaspoon salt
1/2 teaspoon black pepper
   Optional toppings:
   crumbled bacon, sliced
   scallions, sour cream

1. Melt butter in large skillet over medium-high heat. Add onions. Cook and stir 3 to 5 minutes or until softened. Add garlic and cook 15 seconds longer. Transfer to **Crock-Pot®** slow cooker.

2. Add remaining ingredients. Stir well to combine. Cover; cook on LOW 6 to 7 hours or on HIGH 3 hours or until potatoes are tender.

3. Turn **Crock-Pot®** slow cooker to LOW. Process soup, 1 cup at a time, in blender. Return soup to **Crock-Pot®** slow cooker to stay warm. (Or use immersion blender.) Garnish as desired.

PREP TIME: 10 MINUTES

SERVINGS: 4 TO 6

HIGH: 3 HOURS

LOW: 6 TO 7 HOURS

double corn chowder

2 small celery stalks,
   trimmed and chopped
6 ounces Canadian bacon,
   chopped
1 small onion *or* 1 large
   shallot, chopped
1 serrano chile *or* jalapeño
   pepper,* cored, seeded
   and minced
1 cup frozen corn, thawed
1 cup canned hominy
1/4 teaspoon salt, or to taste
1/4 teaspoon crushed dried
   thyme
1/4 teaspoon black pepper
1 cup chicken broth
1 tablespoon flour
1 1/2 cups milk,** divided

*Hot peppers can sting and irritate the skin, so wear rubber gloves when handling peppers and do not touch your eyes.

**For richer chowder, use 3/4 cup milk and 3/4 cup half-and-half.

1. Combine celery, bacon, onion, chile, corn, hominy, salt, thyme and pepper in 4-quart **Crock-Pot®** slow cooker. Add broth. Cover; cook on LOW 5 to 6 hours or on HIGH 3 to 3 1/2 hours.

2. Turn **Crock-Pot®** slow cooker to LOW. Stir together flour and 2 tablespoons milk in small bowl. Stir into corn mixture. Add remaining milk. Cover; cook on LOW 20 minutes.

PREP TIME: 10 MINUTES

SERVINGS: 4

HIGH: 3 TO 3 1/2 HOURS

LOW: 5 TO 6 HOURS

soups & sides

93

gratin potatoes with asiago cheese

PREP TIME: 15 MINUTES

SERVINGS: 4 TO 6

HIGH: 5 TO 6 HOURS

LOW: 7 TO 9 HOURS

6   **slices bacon, cut into 1-inch pieces**
6   **medium baking potatoes, peeled and thinly sliced**
½   **cup grated Asiago cheese**
    Salt and black pepper, to taste
1½   **cups heavy cream**

1. Heat skillet over medium heat until hot. Add bacon. Cook and stir until crispy. Transfer to plate with slotted spoon.

2. Pour bacon fat from skillet into 5- to 6-quart **Crock-Pot®** slow cooker. Layer ¼ of potatoes on bottom of **Crock-Pot®** slow cooker. Sprinkle ¼ of bacon over potatoes and top with ¼ of cheese. Add salt and pepper. Repeat layers. Pour cream over all. Cover; cook on LOW 7 to 9 hours or on HIGH 5 to 6 hours. Adjust salt and pepper, if desired.

chunky ranch potatoes

PREP TIME: 10 MINUTES

SERVINGS: 8

HIGH: 4 TO 6 HOURS

LOW: 7 TO 9 HOURS

3   **pounds medium red potatoes, unpeeled and quartered**
1   **cup water**
½   **cup prepared ranch dressing**
½   **cup grated Parmesan or Cheddar cheese (optional)**
¼   **cup minced chives**

1. Place potatoes in 4-quart **Crock-Pot®** slow cooker. Add water. Cover; cook on LOW 7 to 9 hours or on HIGH 4 to 6 hours, or until potatoes are tender.

2. Stir in ranch dressing, cheese, if desired, and chives. Use spoon to break potatoes into chunks. Serve hot or cold.

soups & sides

gratin potatoes with asiago cheese

wild rice and dried cherry risotto

1 cup dry-roasted salted peanuts
2 tablespoons sesame oil, divided
1 cup chopped onion
6 ounces uncooked wild rice
1 cup diced carrots
1 cup chopped green or red bell pepper
½ cup dried cherries
⅛ to ¼ teaspoon dried pepper flakes
4 cups hot water
¼ cup teriyaki or soy sauce
1 teaspoon salt, or to taste

1. Coat **Crock-Pot®** slow cooker with nonstick cooking spray. Heat large skillet over medium-high heat until hot. Add peanuts. Cook and stir 2 to 3 minutes or until peanuts begin to brown. Transfer peanuts to plate; set aside.

2. Heat 2 teaspoons oil in skillet until hot. Add onions. Cook and stir 6 minutes or until richly browned. Transfer to **Crock-Pot®** slow cooker.

3. Stir in wild rice, carrots, bell pepper, cherries, pepper flakes and water. Cover; cook on HIGH 3 hours.

4. Let stand 15 minutes, uncovered, until rice absorbs liquid. Stir in teriyaki sauce, peanuts, remaining oil and salt.

barley with currants and pine nuts

1 tablespoon unsalted butter
1 small onion, finely chopped
½ cup pearled barley
2 cups chicken broth
½ teaspoon salt, or to taste
¼ teaspoon black pepper
⅓ cup currants
¼ cup pine nuts

1. Melt butter in small skillet over medium-high heat. Add onion. Cook and stir until lightly browned, about 2 minutes. Transfer to 4-quart **Crock-Pot®** slow cooker. Add barley, broth, salt and pepper. Stir in currants. Cover; cook on LOW 3 hours.

2. Stir in pine nuts and serve immediately.

wild rice and dried cherry risotto

spinach gorgonzola corn bread

PREP TIME: 10 MINUTES

SERVINGS: 10 TO 12

HIGH: 1½ HOURS

■ **Tip:** Cook only on HIGH setting for proper crust and texture.

2   boxes (8½ ounces each) corn bread mix
3   eggs
½   cup cream
1   box (10 ounces) frozen chopped spinach, thawed and drained
1   cup crumbled Gorgonzola cheese
1   teaspoon black pepper
    Paprika (optional)

1. Coat **Crock-Pot®** slow cooker with nonstick cooking spray. Mix all ingredients in medium bowl. Pour batter into **Crock-Pot®** slow cooker. Cover; cook on HIGH 1½ hours.

2. Sprinkle top with paprika for more colorful crust, if desired. Let bread cool completely before inverting onto serving platter.

lentils with walnuts

1 cup brown lentils
1 very small onion *or* large shallot, chopped
1 celery stalk, trimmed and chopped
1 large carrot, chopped
¼ teaspoon crushed dried thyme
3 cups chicken broth
 Salt and black pepper, to taste
¼ cup chopped walnuts

1. Combine lentils, onion, celery, carrot, thyme and broth in 4-quart **Crock-Pot®** slow cooker. Cover; cook on HIGH 3 hours. *Do not overcook.* (Lentils should absorb most or all of broth. Slightly tilt **Crock-Pot®** slow cooker to check.)

2. Season with salt and pepper. Spoon lentils into serving bowl and sprinkle on walnuts.

PREP TIME: 10 MINUTES

SERVINGS: 4 TO 6

HIGH: 3 HOURS

■ **Variation:** If desired, top dish with 4 cooked bacon strips cut into bite-size pieces. To serve as a main dish, stir in 1 cup diced cooked ham.

braised sweet and sour cabbage and apples

2 tablespoons unsalted butter
6 cups coarsely shredded red cabbage
1 large sweet apple, peeled, cored and cut into bite-size pieces
3 whole cloves
½ cup raisins
½ cup apple cider
3 tablespoons cider vinegar, divided
2 tablespoons packed dark brown sugar
½ teaspoon salt
¼ teaspoon black pepper

1. Melt butter in very large skillet or shallow pot over medium heat. Add cabbage. Cook and stir 3 minutes until cabbage is glossy. Transfer to 4-quart **Crock-Pot®** slow cooker.

2. Add apple, cloves, raisins, apple cider, 2 tablespoons vinegar, brown sugar, salt and pepper. Cover; cook on LOW 2½ to 3 hours.

3. To serve, remove cloves and stir in remaining 1 tablespoon vinegar.

PREP TIME: 15 MINUTES

SERVINGS: 4 TO 6

LOW: 2½ TO 3 HOURS

soups & sides

99

cornbread stuffing with sausage and green apples

PREP TIME: 20 MINUTES

SERVINGS: 8 TO 12

HIGH: 3 TO 3½ HOURS

■ **Tip:** Consider using your **Crock-Pot®** slow cooker as an extra "oven" or "burner" for holiday entertaining. For example, the **Crock-Pot®** slow cooker can cook the stuffing while the holiday turkey is in the oven.

1   package (16 ounces) honey cornbread mix, plus ingredients to prepare mix
2   cups cubed French bread
1½   pounds mild Italian sausage, casings removed
1   onion, finely chopped
1   green apple, peeled, cored and diced
2   stalks celery, finely chopped
¼   teaspoon dried sage
¼   teaspoon dried rosemary
¼   teaspoon dried thyme
½   teaspoon salt
¼   teaspoon black pepper
3   cups chicken broth
2   tablespoons chopped parsley (optional)

1. Mix and bake cornbread according to package directions. When cool, cover with plastic wrap and set aside overnight.*

2. Coat 5- to 6-quart **Crock-Pot®** slow cooker with nonstick cooking spray. Preheat oven to 350°F. Cut cornbread into 1-inch cubes. Spread cornbread and French bread on baking sheet. Toast in oven about 20 minutes or until dry.

3. Meanwhile, heat medium skillet over medium heat until hot. Add sausage. Cook and stir until browned. Transfer sausage to **Crock-Pot®** slow cooker with slotted spoon.

4. Add onion, apple and celery to skillet. Cook and stir 5 minutes or until softened. Stir in sage, rosemary, thyme, salt and pepper. Transfer mixture to **Crock-Pot®** slow cooker

5. Add bread cubes and stir gently to combine. Pour broth over mixture. Cover; cook on HIGH 3 to 3½ hours or until liquid is absorbed. Garnish with parsley, if desired.

Or purchase prepared 8-inch square pan of cornbread. Proceed as directed.

soups & sides

supper squash medley

PREP TIME: 15 TO
20 MINUTES

SERVINGS: 8 TO 10

LOW: 6½ HOURS

2   butternut squash, peeled, seeded and diced
1   can (28 ounces) tomatoes, undrained
1   can (15 ounces) corn, drained
2   onions, chopped
2   green bell peppers, chopped
2   teaspoons minced garlic
2   green chilies, chopped
1   cup chicken broth
1   teaspoon salt
½   teaspoon black pepper
1   can (6 ounces) tomato paste

1. Combine squash, tomatoes with juice, corn, onions, bell peppers, garlic, chilies, broth, salt and black pepper in **Crock-Pot®** slow cooker. Cover; cook on LOW 6 hours.

2. Remove about ½ cup cooking liquid and blend with tomato paste. Add back to **Crock-Pot®** slow cooker and stir well. Cook 30 minutes or until slightly thickened and heated through.

■ **Tip:** Root vegetables such as potatoes can sometimes take longer to cook in a **Crock-Pot®** slow cooker than meat. When possible, place evenly cut vegetables along the sides of the **Crock-Pot®** slow cooker or allow extra time for vegetarian dishes.

soups & sides

down-home squash casserole

■ **Tip:** Defrost meat and vegetables before cooking them in the **Crock-Pot®** slow cooker.

4   cups cornbread stuffing mix (half of 16-ounce package)
½   cup (1 stick) butter, melted
1   can (10¾ ounces) cream of chicken soup
¾   cup mayonnaise
¼   cup milk
¼   teaspoon poultry seasoning *or* rubbed sage
3   medium yellow squash, cut into ½-inch slices (about 1 pound total)
1½ cups frozen seasoning-blend* vegetables, thawed

Seasoning-blend vegetables are a mixture of chopped bell peppers, onions and celery. If you're unable to find these vegetables, use ½ cup of each fresh vegetable.

1. Coat 5-quart **Crock-Pot®** slow cooker with nonstick cooking spray. Combine stuffing and butter in large bowl, and toss gently to coat stuffing thoroughly. Place ⅔ of stuffing in **Crock-Pot®** slow cooker. Place remaining stuffing on plate; set aside.

2. Combine soup, mayonnaise, milk and poultry seasoning in same large bowl. Add squash and vegetables and stir until coated thoroughly. Pour mixture over stuffing mix in **Crock-Pot®** slow cooker. Sprinkle on remaining stuffing evenly. Cover; cook on LOW 4 hours or until squash is tender.

3. Turn off **Crock-Pot®** slow cooker. Uncover and let stand 15 minutes before serving.

soups & sides

pesto rice and beans

2 cans (15 ounces each) Great Northern beans, rinsed and drained

2 cans (14 ounces each) chicken broth

1½ cups uncooked converted long-grain rice

3 cups frozen cut green beans, thawed and drained

1 cup prepared pesto
  Grated Parmesan cheese (optional)

1. Combine beans, broth and rice in 5- to 6-quart **Crock-Pot®** slow cooker. Cover; cook on LOW 2 hours.

2. Stir in green beans. Cover; cook 1 hour or until rice and beans are tender.

3. Turn off **Crock-Pot®** slow cooker and transfer stoneware to heatproof surface. Stir in pesto and Parmesan cheese, if desired. Let stand, covered, 5 minutes or until cheese is melted. Serve immediately.

| PREP TIME: 5 MINUTES |
| SERVINGS: 16 |
| LOW: 3 HOURS |

lemon and tangerine glazed carrots

PREP TIME: 15 MINUTES

SERVINGS: 10 TO 12

HIGH: 1 TO 3 HOURS

LOW: 4 TO 5 HOURS

6 cups sliced carrots
1½ cups apple juice
6 tablespoons butter
¼ cup packed brown sugar
2 tablespoons grated lemon peel
2 tablespoons grated tangerine peel
½ teaspoon salt
Chopped fresh parsley (optional)

Combine all ingredients in 4-quart **Crock-Pot®** slow cooker. Cover; cook on LOW 4 to 5 hours or on HIGH 1 to 3 hours. Garnish with chopped parsley, if desired.

tarragon carrots in white wine

PREP TIME: 10 MINUTES

SERVINGS: 6 TO 8

HIGH: 1½ TO 2 HOURS

LOW: 2½ TO 3 HOURS

½ cup chicken broth
½ cup dry white wine
1 tablespoon lemon juice
1 tablespoon minced fresh tarragon
2 teaspoons finely chopped green onions
1½ teaspoons chopped flat-leaf parsley
1 clove garlic, minced
1 teaspoon salt
8 medium carrots, peeled and cut into matchsticks
2 tablespoons melba toast, crushed
2 tablespoons cold water

1. Combine broth, wine, lemon juice, tarragon, onions, parsley, garlic and salt in 4-quart **Crock-Pot®** slow cooker. Add carrots; stir well to combine. Cover; cook on LOW 2½ to 3 hours or on HIGH 1½ to 2 hours.

2. Turn **Crock-Pot®** slow cooker to LOW. Dissolve toast crumbs in water and add to carrots. Cover; cook 10 minutes longer or until thickened.

soups & sides

lemon and tangerine glazed carrots

lemon-dilled parsnips and turnips

PREP TIME: 15 MINUTES

SERVINGS: 8 TO 10

HIGH: 1 TO 3 HOURS

LOW: 3 TO 4 HOURS

2 cups chicken broth
¼ cup chopped green onions
4 tablespoons lemon juice
4 tablespoons dried dill
1 teaspoon minced garlic
4 turnips, peeled and cut into ½-inch pieces
3 parsnips, peeled and cut into ½-inch pieces
4 tablespoons cornstarch
¼ cup cold water

1. Combine broth, green onions, lemon juice, dill and garlic in **Crock-Pot®** slow cooker.

2. Add turnips and parsnips; stir well to combine. Cover; cook on LOW 3 to 4 hours or on HIGH 1 to 3 hours, or until vegetables are tender.

3. Turn **Crock-Pot®** slow cooker to HIGH. Dissolve cornstarch in water. Add to **Crock-Pot®** slow cooker; stir well to combine. Cover; cook 15 minutes longer or until thickened.

simmered napa cabbage with dried apricots

PREP TIME: 10 MINUTES

SERVINGS: 4

HIGH: 2 TO 3 HOURS

LOW: 5 TO 6 HOURS

4 cups napa cabbage *or* green cabbage, cored, cleaned and sliced thin
1 cup chopped dried apricots
¼ cup clover honey
2 tablespoons orange juice
½ cup dry red wine
Salt and black pepper, to taste
Grated orange peel (optional)

1. Combine cabbage and apricots in **Crock-Pot®** slow cooker. Toss to mix well.

2. Combine honey and orange juice, mixing until smooth. Drizzle over cabbage. Add wine. Cover; cook on LOW 5 to 6 hours or on HIGH 2 to 3 hours, or until cabbage is tender.

3. Season with salt and pepper. Garnish with orange peel, if desired.

soups & sides

lemon-dilled parsnips and turnips

sweet-spiced sweet potatoes

2   pounds sweet potatoes, peeled and cut into ½-inch pieces
¼   cup packed dark brown sugar
1   teaspoon ground cinnamon
½   teaspoon ground nutmeg
⅛   teaspoon salt
2   tablespoons butter, cut into small pieces
1   teaspoon vanilla

1. Combine potatoes, brown sugar, cinnamon, nutmeg and salt in **Crock-Pot®** slow cooker; mix well. Cover; cook on LOW 7 hours or on HIGH 4 hours.

2. Add butter and vanilla; gently stir to blend.

blue cheese potatoes

2   pounds red potatoes, peeled and cut into ½-inch pieces
1¼ cups chopped green onions, divided
2   tablespoons olive oil, divided
1   teaspoon dried basil
½   teaspoon salt
¼   teaspoon black pepper
2   ounces crumbled blue cheese

1. Layer potatoes, 1 cup green onions, 1 tablespoon oil, basil, salt and pepper in **Crock-Pot®** slow cooker. Cover; cook on LOW 7 hours or on HIGH 4 hours.

2. Turn **Crock-Pot®** slow cooker to HIGH. Gently stir in cheese and remaining 1 tablespoon oil. Cook 5 minutes longer to allow flavors to blend. Transfer potatoes to serving platter and top with remaining ¼ cup green onions.

soups & sides

sweet-spiced sweet potatoes

oriental golden barley with cashews

PREP TIME: 20 MINUTES

SERVINGS: 4

HIGH: 2 TO 3 HOURS

LOW: 4 TO 5 HOURS

2 tablespoons unsalted butter
1 cup hulled barley, sorted
3 cups vegetable broth
1 cup chopped celery
1 green bell pepper, cored, seeded and chopped
1 yellow onion, minced
1 clove garlic, minced
¼ teaspoon black pepper
¼ cup finely chopped cashews

1. Heat skillet over medium heat until hot. Add butter and barley. Cook and stir about 10 minutes or until barley is slightly browned. Transfer to **Crock-Pot®** slow cooker.

2. Add broth, celery, bell pepper, onion, garlic and black pepper. Stir well to combine. Cover; cook on LOW 4 to 5 hours or on HIGH 2 to 3 hours, or until barley is tender and liquid is absorbed.

3. To serve, garnish with cashews.

slow-roasted potatoes

PREP TIME: 5 MINUTES

SERVINGS: 3 TO 4

HIGH: 4 HOURS

LOW: 7 HOURS

16 small new potatoes
3 tablespoons butter, cut into small pieces
1 teaspoon paprika
½ teaspoon salt
¼ teaspoon garlic powder
Black pepper, to taste

1. Combine potatoes, butter, paprika, salt, garlic powder and pepper in **Crock-Pot®** slow cooker; mix well. Cover; cook on LOW 7 hours or on HIGH 4 hours.

2. Transfer potatoes with slotted spoon to serving dish; cover to keep warm. Add 1 to 2 tablespoons water to cooking liquid. Stir until well blended. Pour mixture over potatoes before serving.

soups & sides

oriental golden barley with cashews

orange-spiced sweet potatoes

PREP TIME: 15 MINUTES

SERVINGS: 8

HIGH: 2 HOURS

LOW: 4 HOURS

2   **pounds sweet potatoes, peeled and diced**
½   **cup packed dark brown sugar**
½   **cup (1 stick) butter, cut into small pieces**
1   **teaspoon ground cinnamon**
½   **teaspoon ground nutmeg**
½   **teaspoon grated orange peel**
    Juice of 1 medium orange
¼   **teaspoon salt**
1   **teaspoon vanilla**
    Chopped toasted pecans* (optional)

*To toast pecans, spread in single layer in heavy-bottomed skillet. Cook over medium heat 1 to 2 minutes, stirring frequently, until nuts are lightly browned. Remove from skillet immediately. Cool before using.

Place all ingredients, except pecans, in **Crock-Pot®** slow cooker. Cover; cook on LOW 4 hours or on HIGH 2 hours, or until potatoes are tender. Garnish with pecans, if desired.

■ **Variation:** For a creamy dish, mash potatoes with a hand masher or electric mixer, and add ¼ cup milk or whipping cream for moist consistency. Sprinkle with cinnamon-sugar, and sprinkle on toasted pecans, if desired.

easy
entertaining

entertaining

provençal lemon and olive chicken

2 cups chopped onion
8 skinless chicken thighs (about 2½ pounds)
1 lemon, thinly sliced and seeds removed
1 cup pitted green olives
1 tablespoon olive brine from jar *or* white vinegar
2 teaspoons herbes de Provence
1 bay leaf
½ teaspoon salt
⅛ teaspoon black pepper
1 cup chicken broth
½ cup minced fresh parsley

1. Place onion in 4-quart **Crock-Pot®** slow cooker. Arrange chicken thighs over onion. Place lemon slice on each thigh. Add olives, brine, herbes de Provence, bay leaf, salt and pepper. Slowly pour in chicken broth.

2. Cover; cook on LOW 5 to 6 hours or on HIGH 3 to 3½ hours, or until chicken is tender. Stir in parsley before serving.

PREP TIME: 15 MINUTES

SERVINGS: 8

HIGH: 3 TO 3½ HOURS

LOW: 5 TO 6 HOURS

■ **Note:** To skin chicken easily, grasp skin with paper towel and pull away. Repeat with fresh paper towel for each piece of chicken, discarding skins and towels.

pork loin stuffed with stone fruits

PREP TIME: 20 MINUTES

SERVINGS: 8 TO 10

HIGH: 2 TO 3 HOURS

LOW: 5 TO 6 HOURS

■ **Tip:** To butterfly a roast means to split the meat down the center without cutting all the way through. This allows the meat to be spread open so a filling can be added.

1 **boneless pork loin roast (about 4 pounds)**
Salt and black pepper, to taste
2 **tablespoons vegetable oil**
2 **tablespoons butter**
1 **onion, chopped**
½ **cup Madeira or sherry wine**
1½ **cups dried stone fruits (½ cup each plums, peaches and apricots)**
2 **cloves garlic, minced**
¾ **teaspoon salt**
½ **teaspoon black pepper**
¼ **teaspoon dried thyme**
1 **tablespoon olive oil**
Kitchen string, cut into 15-inch lengths

1. Coat 5- to 6-quart **Crock-Pot®** slow cooker with nonstick cooking spray. Season pork with salt and pepper, to taste. Heat oil in large skillet over medium-high heat oil until hot. Sear pork on all sides, turning as it browns. Transfer to cutting board; let stand until cool enough to handle.

2. Melt butter in same skillet over medium heat. Add onion. Cook and stir until translucent. Add Madeira. Cook 2 to 3 minutes until mixture reduces slightly. Stir in dried fruit, garlic, salt, pepper and thyme. Cook 1 minute longer. Remove skillet from heat.

3. Cut strings from roast, if any. Butterfly roast lengthwise (use sharp knife to cut meat; cut to within 1½ inches of edge). Spread roast flat on cutting board, browned side down. Spoon fruit mixture onto pork roast. Bring sides together to close roast. Slide kitchen string under roast and tie roast shut, allowing 2 inches between ties. If any fruit escapes, push back gently. Place roast in **Crock-Pot®** slow cooker. Pour olive oil over roast. Cover; cook on LOW 5 to 6 hours or on HIGH 2 to 3 hours, or until roast is tender.

4. Transfer roast to cutting board and let stand 10 minutes. Pour cooking liquid into small saucepan (strain through fine-mesh sieve first, if desired). Cook over high heat about 3 minutes to reduce sauce. Add salt and pepper to sauce, if desired. Slice roast and serve with sauce.

merlot'd beef and sun-dried tomato portobello ragoût

PREP TIME: 20 MINUTES

SERVINGS: 8

HIGH: 4 TO 5 HOURS

LOW: 8 TO 9 HOURS

■ **Tip:** Consommé is just clarified broth. If you can't find canned beef consommé, you may substitute beef broth.

1   jar (7 ounces) sun-dried tomatoes in oil, drained, 3 tablespoons oil reserved
1   boneless chuck roast, cut into 1½-inch pieces (about 3 pounds)
1   can (10½ ounces) beef consommé, undiluted
6   ounces sliced portobello mushrooms
1   medium green bell pepper, cut into thin strips
1   medium orange or yellow bell pepper, cut into thin strips
1   medium onion, cut into 8 wedges
2   teaspoons dried oregano
½   teaspoon salt
¼   teaspoon garlic powder
½   cup Merlot or other red wine
2   tablespoons Worcestershire sauce
1   tablespoon balsamic vinegar
1   tablespoon cornstarch
    Salt and black pepper, to taste
    Mashed potatoes, rice or egg noodles

1. Heat 1 tablespoon reserved oil from sun-dried tomatoes in large skillet over medium-high heat until hot. Add ⅓ of beef and brown on all sides. Transfer to 5-quart **Crock-Pot®** slow cooker. Repeat with remaining oil and beef.

2. Add consommé to skillet. Cook and stir, scraping bottom to loosen browned bits. Pour mixture over beef. Add sun-dried tomatoes, mushrooms, bell peppers, onion, oregano, salt and garlic powder to **Crock-Pot®** slow cooker.

3. Combine Merlot and Worcestershire sauce in small bowl; reserve ¼ cup. Gently stir remaining Merlot mixture into **Crock-Pot®** slow cooker. Cover; cook on LOW 8 to 9 hours or on HIGH 4 to 5 hours, or until beef is tender.

4. Turn **Crock-Pot®** slow cooker to HIGH. Stir vinegar and cornstarch into reserved ¼ cup Merlot mixture until cornstarch is dissolved. Add to **Crock-Pot®** slow cooker. Stir until well blended. Cover; cook on HIGH 15 minutes longer or until thickened slightly. Add salt and pepper, if desired. Serve over mashed potatoes.

entertaining

indian-style apricot chicken

PREP TIME: 15 MINUTES

SERVINGS: 4 TO 6

HIGH: 3 TO 4 HOURS

LOW: 5 TO 6 HOURS

■ Note: To skin chicken easily, grasp skin with paper towel and pull away. Repeat with fresh paper towel for each piece of chicken, discarding skins and towels.

6   skinless chicken thighs, rinsed and patted dry
¼   teaspoon salt
¼   teaspoon black pepper
1   tablespoon vegetable oil
1   large onion, chopped
2   cloves garlic, minced
2   tablespoons grated fresh ginger
½   teaspoon ground cinnamon
⅛   teaspoon ground allspice
1   can (14½ ounces) diced tomatoes, undrained
1   cup chicken broth
1   package (8 ounces) dried apricots
1   pinch saffron threads (optional)
   Hot basmati rice
2   tablespoons chopped fresh parsley

1. Coat 5-quart **Crock-Pot®** slow cooker with nonstick cooking spray. Season chicken with salt and pepper. Heat oil in large skillet over medium-high heat until hot. Brown chicken on all sides. Transfer to **Crock-Pot®** slow cooker.

2. Add onion to skillet. Cook and stir 3 to 5 minutes or until translucent. Stir in garlic, ginger, cinnamon and allspice. Cook and stir 15 to 30 seconds longer or until mixture is fragrant. Add tomatoes with juice and broth. Cook 2 to 3 minutes or until mixture is heated through. Pour into **Crock-Pot®** slow cooker.

3. Add apricots and saffron, if desired. Cover; cook on LOW 5 to 6 hours or on HIGH 3 to 4 hours, or until chicken is tender. Add salt and pepper, if desired. Serve with basmati rice and garnish with chopped parsley.

entertaining

sirloin tips with caramelized onion brandy sauce

PREP TIME: 10 MINUTES

SERVINGS: 4

LOW: 6 TO 8 HOURS

■ **Tip:** To enhance the flavor and appearance of this dish, brown the meat first. Heat oil in a skillet until it's hot, then brown the meat in batches, if necessary, before adding it to the **Crock-Pot®** slow cooker.

3 tablespoons all-purpose flour
½ teaspoon salt
½ teaspoon crushed black peppercorns
1½ pounds beef sirloin tips, cut into 2-inch pieces
½ cup beef broth
3 tablespoons brandy
1 teaspoon Worcestershire sauce
1 clove garlic, minced
2 tablespoons butter, melted
1 tablespoon packed brown sugar
¼ teaspoon ground red pepper
1 medium sweet onion, thinly sliced and separated into rings
¼ cup heavy cream
Cooked wild rice or mashed potatoes
½ cup Gorgonzola cheese, crumbled
2 tablespoons finely chopped flat-leaf parsley

1. Combine flour, salt and peppercorns in large resealable plastic food storage bag. Add beef and shake to coat. Transfer to **Crock-Pot®** slow cooker.

2. Combine broth, brandy, Worcestershire sauce and garlic in small bowl. Pour over beef.

3. Combine butter, brown sugar and red pepper in small bowl. Add onion and toss to coat. Transfer to **Crock-Pot®** slow cooker. Cover; cook on LOW 6 to 8 hours.

4. Turn **Crock-Pot®** slow cooker to HIGH. Stir in heavy cream. Cover; cook 15 minutes longer.

5. Serve beef and sauce over wild rice, if desired, and garnish with cheese and parsley.

dijon chicken thighs with artichoke sauce

⅓ cup Dijon mustard
2 tablespoons chopped garlic
½ teaspoon dried tarragon
2½ pounds chicken thighs (about 8), skinned
1 cup chopped onion
1 cup sliced mushrooms
1 jar (12 ounces) quartered marinated artichoke hearts, undrained
¼ cup chopped fresh parsley

1. Combine mustard, garlic and tarragon in large bowl. Add chicken thighs and toss to coat. Transfer to 4- to 6-quart **Crock-Pot®** slow cooker.

2. Add onion, mushrooms and artichokes with liquid. Cover; cook on LOW 6 to 8 hours or on HIGH 4 hours, or until chicken is tender. Stir in parsley just before serving.

PREP TIME: 10 MINUTES

SERVINGS: 8

HIGH: 4 HOURS

LOW: 6 TO 8 HOURS

■ **Serving suggestion:** Serve with hot fettuccine that has been tossed with butter and parsley.

■ **Note:** To skin chicken easily, grasp skin with paper towel and pull away. Repeat with fresh paper towel for each piece of chicken, discarding skins and towels.

entertaining

sicilian steak pinwheels

PREP TIME: 20 TO
25 MINUTES

SERVINGS: 4 TO 6

LOW: 6 HOURS

¾ pound mild or hot Italian sausage, casings removed
1¾ cups fresh bread crumbs
¾ cup grated Parmesan cheese
2 eggs
3 tablespoons minced parsley, plus additional for garnish
1½ to 2 pounds round steak
1 cup frozen peas
  Kitchen string, cut into 15-inch lengths
1 cup tomato pasta sauce
1 cup beef broth

1. Coat 6-quart **Crock-Pot®** slow cooker with nonstick cooking spray. Mix sausage, bread crumbs, cheese, eggs and 3 tablespoons parsley in large bowl until well blended; set aside.

2. Place round steak between 2 large sheets of plastic wrap. Using tenderizer mallet or back of skillet, pound steak until meat is about ⅜ inch thick. Remove top layer of plastic wrap. Spread sausage mixture over steak. Press frozen peas into sausage mixture. Lift edge of plastic wrap at short end to begin rolling steak. Roll up completely. Tie at 2-inch intervals with kitchen string. Transfer to **Crock-Pot®** slow cooker.

3. Combine pasta sauce and broth in medium bowl. Pour over meat. Cover; cook on LOW 6 hours or until meat is tender and sausage is cooked through.

4. Transfer steak to serving platter. Let stand 20 minutes before removing string and slicing. Meanwhile, skim and discard excess fat from sauce. Serve steak slices with sauce.

citrus mangoretto chicken

4 boneless, skinless chicken breasts (about 1 pound)
1 large ripe mango, peeled and diced
3 tablespoons freshly squeezed lime juice
1 tablespoon grated lime peel
¼ cup amaretto liqueur
1 tablespoon chopped fresh rosemary *or* 1 teaspoon crushed dried rosemary
1 cup chicken broth
1 tablespoon water
2 teaspoons cornstarch

1. Place 2 chicken breasts side by side on bottom of **Crock-Pot®** slow cooker.

2. Combine mango, lime juice, lime peel, amaretto and rosemary in medium bowl. Spread half of mango mixture over chicken in **Crock-Pot®** slow cooker. Lay remaining 2 chicken breasts on top crosswise, and spread with remaining mango mixture. Carefully pour broth around edges of chicken. Cover; cook on LOW 3 to 4 hours.

3. Combine water and cornstarch. Stir into cooking liquid. Cook 15 minutes longer or until sauce has thickened. Serve mango and sauce over chicken.

PREP TIME: 15 MINUTES

SERVINGS: 4

LOW: 3 TO 4 HOURS

■ **Variation:** For a refreshing change, chill the cooked chicken and sauce. Slice the chicken and serve it over salad greens, drizzling the sauce on top.

entertaining

125

chipotle rock cornish game hens

PREP TIME: 15 MINUTES

SERVINGS: 4

HIGH: 3½ TO 4½ HOURS

■ **Tip:** Chipotle peppers can be very spicy. Until you know how much spiciness you prefer, use the smaller quantities recommended in recipes. You can always add more the next time you prepare the recipe.

3   small carrots, cut into ½-inch rounds
3   stalks celery, cut into ½-inch pieces
1   onion, chopped
1   can (7 ounces) chipotle peppers in adobo sauce, divided
2   cups prepared cornbread stuffing*
4   Rock Cornish game hens (about 1½ pounds each)
    Salt and black pepper, to taste
    Fresh parsley (optional)

*Or use Cornbread Stuffing with Sausage and Green Apples (recipe on page 100).

1. Coat 5- to 6-quart **Crock-Pot®** slow cooker with nonstick cooking spray. Add carrots, celery and onion.

2. Pour canned chipotles into small bowl. Finely chop 1 chipotle pepper. Remove remaining peppers from adobo sauce and reserve for another use. Mix ½ of chopped chipotle pepper into prepared stuffing. Add remaining ½ of chopped chipotle pepper to adobo sauce.**

3. Rinse and dry hens, removing giblets, if any. Season with salt and pepper inside and out. Fill each hen with about ½ cup stuffing. Rub adobo sauce onto hens. Place in **Crock-Pot®** slow cooker, arranging hens neck down and legs up. Cover; cook on HIGH 3½ to 4½ hours or until hens are cooked through and tender.

4. Transfer hens to serving platter. Remove vegetables with slotted spoon and arrange around hens. Garnish with parsley, if desired. Spoon cooking juices over hens and vegetables, if desired.

**For spicier flavor, use 1 chipotle pepper in stuffing and 1 chipotle pepper in sauce.

moroccan-style lamb shoulder chops with couscous

PREP TIME: 15 MINUTES

SERVINGS: 4

HIGH: 3½ TO 4 HOURS

■ **Tip:** Adding fresh lemon juice just before serving enhances the flavor of many dishes. Try it with other dishes prepared in your **Crock-Pot®** slow cooker.

4 **lamb blade chops (about 2½ pounds)**
Salt and black pepper, to taste
1 **tablespoon olive oil**
1 **onion, chopped**
1 **clove garlic, minced**
1 **teaspoon grated fresh ginger**
¼ **teaspoon ground cinnamon**
½ **teaspoon turmeric**
½ **teaspoon salt**
¼ **teaspoon black pepper**
1 **bay leaf**
1 **can (14½ ounces) diced tomatoes, undrained**
1 **cup canned chickpeas, rinsed and drained**
½ **cup water**
2 **tablespoons lemon juice**
Hot cooked couscous
Lemon wedges (optional)

1. Coat 5- to 6-quart **Crock-Pot®** slow cooker with nonstick cooking spray. Season lamb chops with salt and pepper to taste. Heat oil in large skillet over medium-high heat until hot. Add lamb chops and brown on all sides. Transfer to **Crock-Pot®** slow cooker.

2. Add onions to skillet. Cook and stir 2 to 3 minutes or until translucent. Add garlic, ginger, cinnamon, turmeric, salt, pepper and bay leaf. Cook and stir 30 seconds longer. Stir in tomatoes with juice, chickpeas, water and lemon juice. Simmer 2 minutes. Pour mixture over lamb. Cover; cook on HIGH 3½ to 4 hours or until lamb is tender.

3. Add salt and pepper, if desired. Serve lamb chops over couscous with sauce and vegetables. Serve with lemon wedges, if desired.

easy cheesy aruban-inspired chicken

PREP TIME: 15 MINUTES

SERVINGS: 4

HIGH: 3 TO 4 HOURS

■ **Tip:** Skinless chicken is best for dishes prepared in the **Crock-Pot**® slow cooker because the skin can shrivel and curl during cooking, unless browned first.

1 can (14½ ounces) diced tomatoes in sauce
½ cup chicken broth
¼ cup ketchup
2 teaspoons yellow mustard
1 teaspoon Worcestershire sauce
¾ teaspoon hot sauce
3 cloves garlic, crushed
½ teaspoon salt
¼ teaspoon pepper
1 large onion, thinly sliced
1 large green bell pepper, seeded, cored and thinly sliced
¼ cup sliced black olives
¼ cup raisins
1 tablespoon capers
4 to 6 chicken thighs *or* 4 boneless, skinless breasts
1½ cups (6 ounces) shredded Edam or Gouda cheese
2 tablespoons chopped flat-leaf parsley
Hot cooked rice (optional)

1. Coat **Crock-Pot**® slow cooker with nonstick cooking spray. Add tomatoes in sauce, broth, ketchup, mustard, Worcestershire sauce, hot sauce, garlic, salt and pepper. Stir well to combine.

2. Add onion, bell pepper, olives, raisins and capers. Stir well to combine.

3. Add chicken. Spoon sauce mixture over chicken until well coated. Cover; cook on HIGH 3 to 4 hours or until chicken is fork-tender.

4. Turn off **Crock-Pot**® slow cooker and uncover. Sprinkle cheese and parsley over chicken. Cover and let stand 3 to 5 minutes or until cheese is melted. Serve over rice, if desired.

pecan and apple stuffed pork chops with apple brandy

PREP TIME: 20 MINUTES

SERVINGS: 4

HIGH: 1½ TO 1¾ HOURS

■ **Tip:** Consider using your **Crock-Pot®** slow cooker as an extra "burner" that doesn't need watching. For example, you can cook this main dish in the **Crock-Pot®** slow cooker while you prepare the sides.

4 thick-cut bone-in pork loin chops (about 12 ounces each)
1 teaspoon salt, divided
½ teaspoon black pepper, divided
2 tablespoons vegetable oil
½ cup diced green apple
½ small onion, minced
¼ teaspoon dried thyme
½ cup apple brandy *or* brandy
⅔ cup cubed white bread
2 tablespoons chopped pecans
4 tablespoons frozen butter
1 cup apple juice

1. Coat **Crock-Pot®** slow cooker with nonstick cooking spray; set aside. Rinse pork chops and pat dry. Season with ½ teaspoon salt and ¼ teaspoon pepper. Heat 2 tablespoons oil in large skillet over medium-high heat until hot. Sear pork chops about 2 minutes on both sides or until browned. Cook in 2 batches, if necessary; set aside.

2. Add apple, onion, thyme, ½ teaspoon salt and ¼ teaspoon pepper to hot skillet and reduce heat to medium. Cook and stir 3 minutes or until onions are translucent. Remove from heat and pour in brandy. Return to medium heat and simmer until most of liquid is absorbed. Stir in bread and pecans, and cook 1 minute longer.

3. Cut each pork chop horizontally with sharp knife to form pocket. Place 1 tablespoon butter into each pocket. Divide stuffing among pork chops. Arrange pork chops in **Crock-Pot®** slow cooker, pocket side up.

4. Pour apple juice around pork chops. Cover; cook on HIGH 1½ to 1¾ hours or until pork is tender.

turkey piccata

PREP TIME: 15 MINUTES

SERVINGS: 4

LOW: 1 HOUR

■ **Tip:** This recipe will also work with chicken strips. Start with boneless, skinless chicken breasts, then follow the recipe as directed.

2½ tablespoons all-purpose flour
¼ teaspoon salt, or to taste
¼ teaspoon black pepper
1 pound turkey breast meat, cut into short strips*
1 tablespoon butter
1 tablespoon olive oil
½ cup chicken broth
2 teaspoons freshly squeezed lemon juice
Grated peel of 1 lemon
2 tablespoons finely chopped parsley
2 cups cooked rice (optional)

You may substitute turkey tenderloins; cut as directed.

1. Combine flour, salt and pepper in resealable plastic food storage bag. Add turkey strips and shake well to coat. Heat butter and oil in large skillet over medium-high heat until hot. Add turkey strips in single layer. Brown on all sides, about 2 minutes per side. Transfer to 5-quart **Crock-Pot®** slow cooker, arranging on bottom in single layer.

2. Pour broth into skillet. Cook and stir to scrape up any browned bits. Pour into **Crock-Pot®** slow cooker. Add lemon juice and peel. Cover; cook on LOW 1 hour. Sprinkle with parsley before serving. Serve over rice, if desired.

deep dark
black coffee'd beef

2 cups sliced mushrooms
1 cup chopped onions
2 teaspoons instant coffee granules
1½ teaspoons chili powder
½ teaspoon black pepper
1 boneless chuck beef roast (about 2 pounds)
1 tablespoon vegetable oil
½ cup water
1 tablespoon Worcestershire sauce
1 teaspoon beef bouillon granules *or* 1 bouillon cube
½ teaspoon garlic powder
¾ teaspoon salt

1. Coat **Crock-Pot®** slow cooker with nonstick cooking spray. Add mushrooms and onions; set aside.

2. Combine coffee granules, chili powder and pepper in small bowl. Rub evenly onto beef. Heat oil in large skillet over medium-high heat until hot. Sear beef on all sides, turning as it browns, about 3 minutes per side. Place beef on vegetables in **Crock-Pot®** slow cooker.

3. Add water, Worcestershire sauce, bouillon, garlic powder and salt. Cover; cook on LOW 8 hours or HIGH 4 hours.

4. Transfer beef to serving platter. Pour cooking liquid through fine-mesh sieve to drain well, reserving liquid and vegetables. Place vegetables over beef. Allow cooking liquid to stand 2 to 3 minutes. Skim and discard excess fat. Serve remaining liquid au jus with beef.

PREP TIME: 15 MINUTES

SERVINGS: 4 TO 6

HIGH: 4 HOURS

LOW: 8 HOURS

■ **Tip:** "Au jus" just means "with juice," and usually refers to the cooking liquid in which meats have cooked. If you prefer a thicker sauce, blend 1 tablespoon cornstarch and 2 tablespoons water. Stir into the cooking liquid and continue cooking until it thickens.

entertaining

chai tea
cherries 'n cream

PREP TIME: 10 MINUTES

SERVINGS: 4

HIGH: 2¼ HOURS

■ **Tip:** Long slow cooking allows flavors and spices to blend in delightful desserts and beverages. Use your **Crock-Pot®** slow cooker to experiment with your favorite mulled wines, spiced teas or hot drinks.

2 cans (15½ ounces each) pitted cherries in pear juice
2 cups water
½ cup orange juice
1 cup sugar
4 cardamom pods
2 cinnamon sticks (broken in half)
1 teaspoon grated orange peel
¼ ounce coarsely chopped candied ginger
4 whole cloves
2 black peppercorns
4 green tea bags
1 container (6 ounces) fat-free black cherry yogurt
1 quart vanilla ice cream
   Mint sprigs (optional)

1. Drain cherries, reserving juice; set cherries aside. Combine reserved pear juice, water and orange juice in **Crock-Pot®** slow cooker. Mix in sugar, cardamom, cinnamon, orange peel, ginger, cloves and peppercorns. Cover; cook on HIGH 1¾ hours.

2. Remove spices with slotted spoon and discard. Stir in tea bags and cherries. Cover; cook on HIGH 30 minutes.

3. Remove and discard tea bags. Remove cherries from liquid; set aside. Let liquid cool until warm. Whisk in yogurt until smooth.

4. To serve, divide warm cherries and yogurt sauce among 8 wide-brim wine or cocktail glasses or fancy bowls. Top each serving with small scoop of softened ice cream; swirl lightly. Garnish with mint, if desired.

spiked sponge cake

■ **Tip:** Allow breads, cakes and puddings to cool at least 5 minutes before scooping or removing them from the **Crock-Pot®** stoneware.

cake

1   package (18.2 ounces) yellow cake mix
1   cup water
½   cup vegetable oil
4   large eggs
1   tablespoon grated orange peel
1   package (6 ounces) golden raisins and cherries or other chopped dried fruit (about 1 cup)

sauce

1   cup chopped pecans
½   cup sugar
½   cup butter
¼   cup bourbon *or* apple juice

1. Generously coat 5-quart **Crock-Pot®** slow cooker with nonstick cooking spray. Cut parchment paper to fit bottom of stoneware* and press into place. Spray paper lightly with nonstick cooking spray.

2. Combine cake mix, water, oil, and eggs in large bowl; stir well. (Batter will be a bit lumpy). Stir in orange peel. Pour ⅔ of batter into **Crock-Pot®** slow cooker. Sprinkle dried fruits evenly over batter. Spoon on remaining batter evenly. Cover; cook on HIGH 1½ to 1¾ hours or until toothpick inserted into center of cake comes out clean.

3. Immediately remove stoneware from cooking base and cool 10 minutes on wire rack. Run flat rubber spatula around outer edges, lifting up the bottom slightly. Invert onto serving plate. Peel off paper.

4. Prepare sauce: Heat large skillet over medium-high heat until hot. Add pecans. Cook and stir 2 to 3 minutes or until pecans begin to brown. Add sugar, butter and bourbon and bring to a boil, stirring constantly. Cook 1 to 2 minutes longer or until sugar has dissolved. Pour sauce over entire cake or spoon sauce over each serving.

*To cut parchment paper to fit, trace around the stoneware bottom, then cut the paper slightly smaller to fit. If parchment paper is unavailable, substitute waxed paper.

the claus's christmas pudding

PREP TIME: 30 TO
35 MINUTES

SERVINGS: 12

LOW: 5½ HOURS

■ **Tip:** Steaming the plum pudding in a "water bath" keeps it moist. The "water bath" technique also works well for flan and cheesecake by providing a moist cooking environment that prevents cracking in the finished desserts.

pudding

2	tablespoons unsalted butter
⅔	cup sweetened dried cranberries
⅔	cup golden raisins
½	cup whole candied red cherries, halved
¾	cup cream sherry
18	slices cranberry or other fruited bread
3	large egg yolks, beaten
1½	cups light cream
⅓	cup granulated sugar
¼	teaspoon kosher salt
1½	teaspoons cherry extract
1	cup white chocolate baking chips
1	cup hot water

sauce

2	large egg yolks, beaten
¼	cup powdered sugar, sifted
2	tablespoons cream sherry
¼	teaspoon vanilla
½	cup whipping cream

1. Preheat oven to 250°F. Generously butter 6½-cup ceramic or glass bowl. Place cranberries and raisins in small bowl; set aside. Place cherries in another bowl. Heat ¾ cup sherry until warm, and pour over cherries; set aside.

2. Place bread slices on baking sheet and bake 5 minutes. Turn and bake 5 minutes longer or until bread is dry. Cool, then cut into ½-inch cubes.

3. For custard, combine 3 egg yolks, light cream, granulated sugar and salt in heavy saucepan. Cook and stir over medium heat until mixture coats metal spoon. Remove from heat. Set saucepan in sink filled with ice water to cool quickly; stir 1 to 2 minutes. Stir in cherry extract. Transfer cooled mixture to large bowl. Fold bread cubes into custard until coated.

4. Drain cherries, reserving sherry. Arrange ¼ of cherries, plus ⅓ cup raisin mixture and ¼ cup baking chips prepared ceramic bowl. Add ¼ of bread cube mixture. Sprinkle with reserved sherry drained from cherries. Repeat layers 3 times, arranging fruit near edges of bowl. Pour remaining reserved sherry drained from cherries over all.

5. Cover bowl with buttered foil, butter side down. Place in **Crock-Pot®** slow cooker. Pour hot water around bowl. Cover; cook on LOW 5½ hours. Remove bowl and let stand on wire rack 10 to 15 minutes before unmolding.

6. Prepare sauce: Combine egg yolks, powdered sugar, 2 tablespoons sherry and vanilla. Beat whipping cream in small bowl until small peaks form. Fold whipped cream into egg yolk mixture. Cover; chill until serving time. Serve with warm pudding.

cinnamon latté

PREP TIME: 5 MINUTES

SERVINGS: 6 TO 8

HIGH: 3 HOURS

6 cups double-strength brewed coffee*
2 cups half-and-half
1 cup sugar
1 teaspoon vanilla
3 cinnamon sticks, plus additional for garnish
Whipped cream (optional)

*Double the amount of coffee grounds normally used to brew coffee. Or, substitute 8 teaspoons instant coffee dissolved in 6 cups boiling water.

1. Blend coffee, half-and-half, sugar and vanilla in 3- to 4-quart **Crock-Pot®** slow cooker. Add cinnamon sticks. Cover; cook on HIGH 3 hours.

2. Remove cinnamon sticks. Serve latté in tall coffee mugs with dollop of whipped cream and cinnamon stick, if desired.

cinn-sational swirl cake

PREP TIME: 5 MINUTES

SERVINGS: 10 TO 12

HIGH: 1½ TO 1¾ HOURS

LOW: 3 TO 4 HOURS

1 box (21.5 ounces) cinnamon swirl cake mix
1 cup sour cream
1 cup cinnamon-flavored baking chips
1 cup water
¾ cup vegetable oil
1 package (4-serving size) instant French vanilla pudding and pie filling mix
Cinnamon ice cream (optional)

1. Coat **Crock-Pot®** slow cooker with nonstick cooking spray. Set cinnamon swirl mix packet aside. Place remaining cake mix in **Crock-Pot®** slow cooker.

2. Add sour cream, cinnamon chips, water and oil; stir well to combine. Batter will be slightly lumpy. Add reserved cinnamon swirl mix, slowly swirling through batter with knife. Cover; cook on LOW 3 to 4 hours or on HIGH 1½ to 1¾ hours, or until toothpick inserted into center of cake comes out clean.

3. Serve warm with cinnamon ice cream, if desired.

cinnamon latté

hot fudge cake

■ **Tip:** Your **Crock-Pot®** slow cooker can become an extra "oven" to help when you're entertaining. For example, the **Crock-Pot®** slow cooker can make this dessert while a holiday roast is in the oven.

1¾ cups packed light brown sugar, divided
2 cups all-purpose flour
3 tablespoons plus ¼ cup unsweetened cocoa powder, divided
2 teaspoons baking powder
1 teaspoon salt
1 cup milk
4 tablespoons (½ stick) butter, melted
1 teaspoon vanilla
3½ cups boiling water
Unsweetened cocoa powder *or* ground sweet chocolate (optional)

1. Coat **Crock-Pot®** slow cooker with nonstick cooking spray or butter. Mix 1 cup brown sugar, flour, 3 tablespoons cocoa powder, baking powder and salt in medium bowl. Stir in milk, butter and vanilla. Mix until well-blended. Pour into **Crock-Pot®** slow cooker.

2. Blend remaining ¾ cup brown sugar and ¼ cup cocoa powder in small bowl. Sprinkle evenly over mixture in **Crock-Pot®** slow cooker. Pour in boiling water. Do not stir.

3. Cover; cook on HIGH 1¼ to 1½ hours or until toothpick inserted into center comes out clean. Allow cake to rest 10 minutes, then invert onto serving platter or scoop into serving dishes. Serve warm; dust with cocoa powder, if desired.

fruit ambrosia with dumplings

PREP TIME: 15 MINUTES

SERVINGS: 4 TO 6

HIGH: 2½ TO 3 HOURS

LOW: 5 TO 6 HOURS

PLUS 30 MINUTES TO
1 HOUR ON HIGH
(FOR DUMPLINGS)

■ **Tip:** If you prefer, you can omit the dumplings and serve this fruit ambrosia over sliced pound cake or angel food cake instead.

4   cups fresh or frozen fruit*
½   cup plus 2 tablespoons granulated sugar, divided
½   cup warm apple or cran-apple juice
2   tablespoons quick-cooking tapioca
1   cup all-purpose flour
1¼   teaspoons baking powder
¼   teaspoon salt
3   tablespoons butter, cut into small pieces
½   cup milk
1   large egg
2   tablespoons light brown sugar, plus additional for garnish
     Vanilla ice cream, whipped cream or fruity yogurt (optional)

Use strawberries, raspberries, blueberries or peaches.

1. Combine fruit, ½ cup granulated sugar, juice and tapioca in **Crock-Pot®** slow cooker; stir to mix well. Cover; cook on LOW 5 to 6 hours or on HIGH 2½ to 3 hours, or until fruit forms thick sauce.

2. Combine flour, remaining 2 tablespoons granulated sugar, baking powder and salt in mixing bowl. Cut in butter using pastry blender or 2 knives until mixture resembles coarse crumbs. Stir together milk and egg in small bowl. Pour milk and egg mixture into flour mixture. Stir until soft dough forms.

3. Turn **Crock-Pot®** slow cooker to HIGH. Drop dough by teaspoonfuls on top of fruit. Sprinkle dumplings with 2 tablespoons brown sugar. Cover; cook 30 minutes to 1 hour or until toothpick inserted in dumplings comes out clean.

4. Sprinkle dumplings with additional brown sugar, if desired. Serve warm. Garnish as desired.

entertaining

cherry delight

PREP TIME: 10 MINUTES

SERVINGS: 8 TO 10

HIGH: 1½ TO 2 HOURS

LOW: 3 TO 4 HOURS

1   can (21 ounces) cherry pie filling
1   package (18¼ ounces) yellow cake mix
½   cup (1 stick) butter, melted
⅓   cup chopped walnuts
    Whipped topping or vanilla ice cream (optional)

1. Place pie filling in **Crock-Pot®** slow cooker.

2. Combine cake mix and butter in medium bowl. Spread evenly over cherry filling. Sprinkle walnuts on top. Cover; cook on LOW 3 to 4 hours or on HIGH 1½ to 2 hours.

3. Spoon into serving dishes, and serve warm with whipped topping or ice cream, if desired.

fresh bosc pear granita

PREP TIME: 15 MINUTES

SERVINGS: 6

HIGH: 2½ TO 3½ HOURS

1   pound fresh Bosc pears, cored, peeled and cubed
1¼   cups water
¼   cup sugar
½   teaspoon ground cinnamon
1   tablespoon lemon juice

1. Place pears, water, sugar, and cinnamon in 3-quart **Crock-Pot®** slow cooker. Cover; cook on HIGH 2½ to 3½ hours or until pears are very soft and tender. Stir in lemon juice.

2. Transfer pears and syrup to blender or food processor and process mixture until smooth. Strain mixture through sieve. Discard any pulp. Pour liquid into 11×9-inch baking pan. Cover tightly with plastic wrap. Place pan in freezer.

3. Stir every hour while freezing, tossing granita with fork. Crush any lumps in mixture as it freezes. Freeze 3 to 4 hours, or until firm. You may keep granita in freezer up to 2 days before serving; toss granita every 6 to 12 hours.

cherry delight

rum and cherry cola fudge spoon cake

PREP TIME: 15 MINUTES

SERVINGS: 8 TO 10

HIGH: 2½ HOURS

■ **Tip:** When mixing cake batter, don't overbeat. Instead, follow all recommended mixing directions.

cake

½	cup cola
½	cup dried sour cherries
1	cup chocolate milk
½	cup (1 stick) unsalted butter, melted
2	teaspoons vanilla
1½	cups all-purpose flour
½	cup ground sweet chocolate
½	cup granulated sugar
2½	teaspoons baking powder
½	teaspoon salt

topping

1¼	cups vanilla cola
¼	cup dark rum
½	cup ground sweet chocolate
½	cup granulated sugar
½	cup packed brown sugar

1. Coat **Crock-Pot®** slow cooker with nonstick cooking spray. Bring cola and dried cherries to a boil in saucepan. Remove from heat; let cherries stand 30 minutes.

2. Combine chocolate milk, melted butter and vanilla in small bowl. Combine flour, ground chocolate, granulated sugar, baking powder and salt in medium bowl; stir to mix well. Make a well in center of dry ingredients; add milk mixture and stir until smooth. Stir cherry mixture into batter. Pour into **Crock-Pot®** slow cooker.

3. Prepare topping: Bring vanilla cola and rum to a boil in saucepan. Remove from heat. Add ground chocolate and sugars; stir until smooth. Gently pour over batter. *Do not stir.* Cover; cook on HIGH 2½ hours or until cake is puffed and top layer has set.

4. Turn off **Crock-Pot®** slow cooker. Let stand, covered, 30 minutes. Serve warm. Garnish as desired.

pineapple rice pudding

1   can (20 ounces) crushed
    pineapple in juice,
    undrained
1   can (13½ ounces)
    coconut milk
1   can (12 ounces) fat-free
    evaporated milk
¾   cup uncooked arborio
    rice
2   eggs, lightly beaten
¼   cup granulated sugar
¼   cup packed light brown
    sugar
½   teaspoon ground
    cinnamon
¼   teaspoon ground
    nutmeg
¼   teaspoon salt
    Toasted coconut* and
    pineapple slices
    (optional)

*To toast coconut, spread evenly on
ungreased baking sheet. Toast in
preheated 350°F oven 5 to 7 minutes,
stirring occasionally, until light golden
brown.

1. Place pineapple with juice,
coconut milk, evaporated milk,
rice, eggs, sugar, brown sugar,
cinnamon, nutmeg and salt into
Crock-Pot® slow cooker; mix
well. Cover; cook on HIGH 3 to
4 hours or until thickened and rice
is tender.

2. Stir until blended. Serve warm
or chilled. Garnish with coconut
and pineapple, if desired.

PREP TIME: 5 MINUTES

SERVINGS: 8

HIGH: 3 TO 4 HOURS

entertaining

151

chocolate malt pudding cake

PREP TIME: 15 MINUTES

SERVINGS: 6 TO 8

HIGH: 2 TO 2½ HOURS

■ **Tip:** Prepare this sweet treat in your **Crock-Pot®** slow cooker during dinner, so you can delight your family and guests with an appetizing warm dessert.

2 tablespoons unsalted butter
1 cup all-purpose flour
½ cup packed brown sugar
2 tablespoons unsweetened cocoa powder
1½ teaspoons baking powder
½ cup milk
2 tablespoons vegetable oil
½ teaspoon almond extract
½ cup coarsely chopped malted milk balls
½ cup semisweet chocolate chips
¾ cup granulated sugar
¼ cup malted milk powder
2 cups boiling water
4 ounces cream cheese, cubed, at room temperature
¼ cup sliced almonds (optional)
Vanilla ice cream (optional)

1. Generously butter **Crock-Pot®** slow cooker. Combine flour, brown sugar, cocoa powder and baking powder in medium bowl. Add milk, oil and almond extract. Stir until smooth.

2. Stir in malted milk balls and chocolate chips. Spread batter evenly in bottom of **Crock-Pot®** slow cooker.

3. Combine granulated sugar and malted milk powder in medium bowl. Mix boiling water and cream cheese in another bowl. Stir into malted milk mixture. Pour evenly over batter in **Crock-Pot®** slow cooker. *Do not stir.* Cover; cook on HIGH 2 to 2½ hours or until toothpick inserted in center comes out clean.

4. Let stand, uncovered, 30 minutes. Spoon into dessert dishes. Garnish with almonds and serve with ice cream, if desired.

brioche and amber rum custard

■ **Tip:** This dessert is delicious when made with any rich egg bread, such as challah.

2 tablespoons unsalted butter
3½ cups heavy cream
4 large eggs
½ cup packed dark brown sugar
⅓ cup amber or light rum
2 teaspoons vanilla
1 loaf (20 to 22 ounces) brioche bread,* torn into pieces or 5 large brioche, cut into thirds
½ cup coarsely chopped pecans
Caramel or butterscotch topping (optional)

If desired, trim and discard heels.

1. Generously coat 5- to 6-quart **Crock-Pot®** slow cooker with butter. Combine cream, eggs, brown sugar, rum and vanilla in large bowl. Stir well to combine.

2. Divide brioche pieces into 4 mounds. Arrange 1 mound in an overlapping fashion in bottom of **Crock-Pot®** slow cooker. Ladle ¼ of cream mixture over brioche. Sprinkle with ⅓ of pecans. Repeat with remaining brioche, cream mixture and nuts.

3. Cover; cook on HIGH 1¾ to 2 hours or on LOW 3 to 3½ hours. Continue cooking until custard is set and tester inserted into center comes out clean.

4. Serve warm. Drizzle with caramel topping, if desired.

bananas foster

PREP TIME: 5 MINUTES

SERVINGS: 12

LOW: 1 TO 2 HOURS

12   **bananas, cut into quarters**
1   **cup flaked coconut**
1   **teaspoon ground cinnamon**
½   **teaspoon salt**
1   **cup dark corn syrup**
⅔   **cup butter, melted**
2   **teaspoons grated lemon peel**
¼   **cup lemon juice**
2   **teaspoons rum**
12   **slices pound cake**
1   **quart vanilla ice cream**

1. Combine bananas and coconut in **Crock-Pot®** slow cooker. Stir together cinnamon, salt, corn syrup, butter, lemon peel, lemon juice and rum in medium bowl. Pour over bananas. Cover; cook on LOW 1 to 2 hours.

2. To serve, arrange bananas on pound cake slices. Top with ice cream and pour on warm sauce.

index